GREAT
OUTDOOR
2 x 4
FURNITURE

GREAT OUTDOOR 2 x 4 FURNITURE

21 Easy Projects to Build

Stevie Henderson with Mark Baldwin

Lark Books
Asheville, North Carolina

Dedication

For the gang at Cannons!

Editor: Deborah Morgenthal
Art Director and Production: Kathleen Holmes
Computer Illustrations and Technical Support: Thomas Stender
Line Drawings: Orrin Lundgren
Photography: Evan Bracken

Library of Congress Cataloging-in-Publication Data

Henderson, Stevie, 1943-

    Great outdoor 2 x 4 furniture : 21 easy projects to build / Stevie Henderson with Mark Baldwin.
        p.   cm.
    Includes index.
    ISBN 1-57990-036-4 (hard). — ISBN 1-57990-047-X (paper)
    1. Outdoor furniture. 2. Woodwork. 3. Garden ornaments and furniture—Design and construction. I. Baldwin, Mark. 1975- II. Title.
    TT197.5.09H46   1998
    684.1'8—dc21

                                                    97-51232
                                                     CIP

10 9 8 7 6 5 4 3 2 1

First Edition

Published by Lark Books
50 College St.
Asheville, NC 28801, US

Distributed by Random House, Inc., in the United States, Canada, the United Kingdom, Europe, and Asia

Distributed in Australia by Capricorn Link (Australia) Pty Ltd., P.O. Box 6651, Baulkham Hills Business Centre, NSW 2153, Australia

Distributed in New Zealand by Tandem Press Ltd., 2 Rugby Rd., Birkenhead, Auckland, New Zealand

Printed in the United States

ISBN 1-57990-036-4 (hard). — ISBN 1-57990-047-X (paper)

CONTENTS

INTRODUCTION

If you have always wanted to build your own outdoor furniture but lacked the woodworking experience, this book is for you! All of the projects contained in these pages are "do-able"— even if you have never built furniture before. If you can imagine yourself nailing one board to another, you can make these projects.

Each of the outdoor pieces has been designed to eliminate tough-to-do woodworking maneuvers and simplify construction so that a beginner can understand. Feel free to pick up that hammer and saw and build one or all of the projects in this book. There's plenty of variety, including a garden chair, a dining table, a potting bench, three types of planters, a lawn bench, a lattice bower, and a hammock stand.

We hope that you will find just the right project for your lawn, garden, deck, or dock. Because we live in Florida, we are outdoors year 'round, and our lawn furniture gets as much use as our indoor furniture. For that reason, we know it's important to build practical and sturdy projects that will last. No matter where you live, we think you'll enjoy building and using the designs in this book.

MATERIALS, TOOLS, AND TECHNIQUES

This book is written for beginning wood-workers who want to build sturdy, good-looking, and practical furniture and accessories for their patio, garden, or lawn. If you have ever held a hammer and know what a nail is, you can build the projects in this book. There is nothing mystical about working with wood. Like any endeavor, it requires some patience and a little introductory knowledge to get started. We suggest that you read through this section before beginning any project.

If you are an accomplished woodworker who works in a fully equipped shop of stationary power tools, please bear in mind that these instructions are geared to the beginner. Many of the procedures in this book don't translate logically or safely to large, stationary power tools. We suggest, therefore, that you alter the instructions to accommodate your more advanced tools and knowledge. Know the capabilities of your tools and don't exceed them.

MATERIALS AND SUPPLIES

By definition, building outdoor furniture requires using materials and finishes that will stand up to the elements. There are lots of options in woods, adhesives, fasteners, and finishes. With a little information, you will be able to make informed choices about the materials and supplies that are available. These choices become easier if you start by defining your personal needs in terms of location, budget, and appearance.

The first thing to consider is where you plan to place your finished project. All outdoor sites are not the same. Will the bench you are building be placed on a covered porch in a moderate climate, or will it sit in the middle of a yard during a Montana snowstorm? Do you want to build an heirloom piece that will last for years—no matter what the cost? Are you building a piece that will be grouped with existing furniture that you would like to match? The answers to questions like these will determine the appropriate wood, adhesive, fasteners, and finish for each woodworking project you undertake.

LUMBER

The two basic classifications of wood are *softwood* and *hardwood*. As the name implies, softwood is usually softer and therefore easier to work with than hardwood. It is also much less expensive. Because of this, softwood is usually a good choice for beginning woodworkers. We built all of the projects in this book with white pine, a readily available softwood. But you could build them with hardwood. Softwood is cut from coniferous trees (evergreens), such as pine, redwood, and cedar. Hardwood comes from deciduous trees, such as oak, maple, cherry, and walnut, which shed their leaves each year.

Because these projects are designed for outdoor use (which doesn't mean you *have* to put them outside!) you will most likely want to use wood that will stand up to life in the great outdoors. Damp weather, insects, and fungi cause wood to deteriorate. Heartwood, the dense, dead wood from the inner core of a tree, repels moisture and insects far more effectively than the sapwood which surrounds it. However, this core wood takes years to develop, and most old-growth trees have been harvested long ago. Today, most commercial lumber consists of second-growth timber that lacks any substantial amount of heartwood.

Some species are naturally resistant to decay and insects. They include white cedar, redwood, black locust, cypress, hemlock, and oak. Douglas

fir and Southern yellow pine, although they are not as resistant to damage, are good choices for outdoor furniture. They are reasonably priced, hard, and durable. They also do well when chemically treated.

You can use untreated pine for these projects, as long as the lumber is thoroughly sealed, painted, and then sealed again. If the piece you are building will be exposed to the elements for any length of time, we recommend that you use a treated pine.

Treated Wood There are two general categories of preservatives used to treat wood— oils, such as creosote and pentachlorophenol solutions in petroleum, and chemical salts that are applied as waterborne solutions. The lumber you purchase will probably be treated with the second method, and is known as *pressure-treated* or *"PT"* wood. Aptly named, the preservatives are forced under pressure into the cells of the wood to protect it from destructive organisms. Lumber treated in this way will last five to ten times longer than untreated lumber.

Pressure-treated lumber is classified by how it will be used: above ground or in contact with the ground. If any portion of the project will come in contact with the ground, I feel safer using the latter classification, even though it is more expensive. Just to make things more complicated, there is also a difference between pressure-treated wood used for decks and buildings, and PT-wood used for general purposes. This information should be printed on a tag stapled to the end grain of the lumber you buy. If not, ask the salesperson to help you determine if you are buying the best treated lumber for your needs. Ratings may simply be labeled LP-2 for aboveground use, and LP-22 for belowground use. If you plan to build a hammock stand and place it directly on the lawn, I recommend that you purchase belowground treated wood.

Please keep in mind that there are chemicals in treated lumber. Always wear a dust mask when you cut treated lumber. Never burn treated-wood scraps. And, if you are concerned about possible skin sensitivities to treated lumber, you may want to wear leather gloves. After handling treated lumber, be sure to wash your hands before eating, and wash your work clothes separately from other laundry.

The ultimate choice of wood will probably be driven by your budget. For each of the materials required for exterior projects, the cost goes up relative to its ability to withstand the onslaught of Mother Nature. Untreated pine will work when correctly finished and placed in a protected area; aboveground treated pine will be fine for projects placed on a patio or deck; belowground treated pine will work for projects placed directly on the ground. Moving up in expense, redwood or cypress work well for all projects, and can be placed directly on the ground.

Wood Selection No matter what grade you purchase, you should inspect each and every board for defects and imperfections. A little extra inspection time in the store will save you hours of frustration later, and will be well worth the effort. Some building-supply outlets will not allow you to hand-select individual boards; I suggest you take your business elsewhere. While it is possible (but extremely time-consuming) to correct some defects in wood, it is simply easier to purchase blemish-free boards in the first place. There is no point in buying wood that is unusable, no matter how cheap the price.

Many large building-supply stores purchase their wood from different suppliers, and that means that, even in the same bin at the same store, the board widths may vary slightly. On the surface (no pun intended), that may not seem like a big deal. But even a difference of 1/64 of an inch in width between two boards will mean that your project will not fit together correctly. So when you purchase wood for a specific project, place the boards together to make certain that they are all exactly the same width.

While you are checking, examine the board for warps, especially *bows* and *cups*. Bowing occurs across the width of the board, and cupping is warpage across the board from edge to edge. If you will be cutting only very short pieces of wood and the warpage is very slight, it probably will not affect your finished project. But if you need longer lengths, search until you find boards that are straight along the entire length. A good method to check for warping or bowing before you buy lumber is

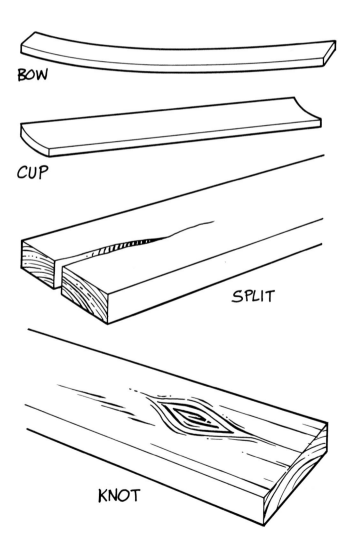

BOW

CUP

SPLIT

KNOT

to place one end of the board on the floor, and look down its length. Then turn the board and look down the edge. Your own eye is the best judge.

Also check for *knots*. Small, tight knots are usually okay—especially for outdoor furniture that you plan to paint. But large knots may become a problem, as they are tough to cut through and also may fall out, leaving you with an unattractive hole in your finished project. Some imperfections can simply be eliminated. If a board is otherwise acceptable, but has a knothole on the end, it is easy enough to simply cut it off. But be sure to purchase extra material to compensate for the loss.

Avoid buying boards that contain *splits*. Splits have a nasty habit of growing lengthwise, ultimately resulting in two narrow and unusable boards. If the split occurs only at one end, you can cut it off, but again, allow extra material for the waste.

When you begin cutting pieces for your project, always cut the longest pieces first. That way, if you inadvertently miscut a piece, that board can be used to cut the short pieces needed in the project. Also re-examine each board before you cut it. If you need a 5-foot piece from a 6-foot board, eliminate the end that has the most defects. During assembly, examine each piece again, and use the best side of each board where it will be seen. Following these steps will save you a lot of time in filling and sanding, and will also give you a better-looking finished project.

Softwood Dimension Lumber Stock from a lumberyard that is *planed* or surfaced to a certain size is called *dimension lumber*. The terms 2 x 4 or 1 x 6 describe wood that has been graded and dimensioned according to predetermined standards. Sizes are given in a three-number *nominal size*, such as 2 x 4 x 8. Sounds simple, right? It would be if a 2 x 4 x 8 really meant that the board was 2 inches thick, 4 inches wide,

and 8 inches long. But such is not the case! Apparently, the sawmills, lumberyards, and building-supply stores have conspired to confuse us: A 2 x 4 is actually 1½ inches thick and 3½ inches wide.

There is a reason for this. When the board is first cut, it is 2 inches thick and 4 inches wide. But wood shrinks after it is cut and dried. Then it is planed on all four sides, which removes up to ½ inch of material in thickness and width. The good news is that the length doesn't change! Listed below are the nominal and the *actual sizes* for softwood lumber:

Nominal Size	Actual Size
1 x 2	¾" x 1½"
1 x 3	¾" x 2½"
1 x 4	¾" x 3½"
1 x 6	¾" x 5½"
1 x 8	¾" x 7¼"
1 x 10	¾" x 9¼"
1 x 12	¾" x 11¼"
2 x 2	1½" x 1½"
2 x 4	1½" x 3½"
2 x 6	1½" x 5½"
2 x 8	1½" x 7¼"
2 x 10	1½" x 9¼"
2 x 12	1½" x 11¼"
4 x 4	3½" x 3½"
4 x 6	3½" x 5½"
6 x 6	5½" x 5½"
8 x 8	7½" x 7½"

Softwood is also graded according to its quality. And, as with anything else, the better the quality, the higher the price. Don't buy better quality than you need for the project you are building. A few imperfections may make your outdoor project look even more rustic (if that is the look you are after). Softwood grades are as follows:

Common Grades

No. 1 common — Contains knots and a few imperfections, but should have no knotholes

No. 2 common — Free of knotholes, but contains some knots

No. 3 common — Contains larger knots and small knotholes

No. 4 common — Used for construction only; contains large knotholes

No. 5 common — Lowest grade of lumber; used only when strength and appearance aren't necessary

Select Grades

B and better (or 1 and 2 clear) — The best and most expensive grades used for the finest furniture projects

C select — May have a few small blemishes

D select — The lowest quality of the better board grades; it has imperfections that can be concealed with paint

Hardwood You can also use hardwood to build any of the projects in this book. White oak, American white ash, boxwood, black locust, and teak work well for outdoor projects. (Teak is an endangered species, so please make sure the wood comes from certified sources.)

If you decide to use a hardwood for your project, it will take some calculating on your part, since hardwood is normally sold in random widths and lengths. Each board is cut from the log as wide and as long as possible. Consequently, hardwood is sold by a measure called the *board foot*. A board foot represents a piece of lumber 1 inch (or less) thick, 12 inches wide, and 1 foot long. Hardwood thicknesses are measured in ¼-inch gradations, expressed as a fraction; a 1¼-inch board is called 5/4-inch stock. The standard thicknesses are ¾, 4/4, 5/4, 6/4, and 8/4. To calculate

board feet, multiply the thickness by the width in inches, then multiply the length in feet and divide by 12.

Plywood As you might guess, plywood is made from several plies of wood that are glued together. Exterior-grade plywood is sold in standard size sheets measuring 4 feet by 8 feet. In some supply stores you can also purchase half-sheets measuring 4 feet by 4 feet. Plywood comes in standard thicknesses of ⅛, ¼, ⅜, ½, ⅝, and ¾ inch.

There are two principal kinds of plywood: *veneer-core* and *lumber-core*. Lumber-core is the higher quality material; its edges can be worked as you would work solid wood. The exposed cut edges of veneer-core plywood must be either filled or covered because they are unsightly.

Plywood is also graded according to the quality of the outer veneer. The grades are A through D, with A representing the best quality. A piece of plywood has two designations, one for each face. For example, an A-D piece has one veneered surface that is A quality and one that is D quality.

Any outdoor project should be built using only exterior-rated plywood. This designation means that the glue between the plies is waterproof. Interior-grade plywood should not be used to construct outdoor projects, as it will warp and split apart when exposed to the elements for even a very short period of time.

Before You Start Before shopping for your materials, please take the time to carefully read the materials and supplies list, the cutting list, and the instructions for that particular project. Each materials list specifies the total number of linear feet of each specific dimension of wood required to make that project. The cutting list itemizes each individual piece you will be cutting to make that project. If the total linear feet of 2 x 4 pine required is 40 feet, and you see in the cutting list that no individual piece of 2 x 4 wood needs to be longer than 6 feet, then you can purchase five 8-foot lengths, four 10-foot lengths, and so on. When you arrive at the lumberyard or building-supply store you may find that the 8-foot lengths of wood are of lesser quality than the 6-foot lengths. In this case, you could then buy seven 6-foot lengths, and have a little left over.

It is also wise to keep transportation capabilities in mind. If you own (or can borrow) a pickup truck to transport your materials, board lengths are not a factor. But it is pretty difficult to get a 12-foot length of wood into a Corvette for the trip home. Most building-supply stores will be happy to give you one free cut on an individual piece of lumber, but some charge a fee.

Unless you have chosen a very expensive wood to build your project, it makes sense to slightly overbuy your materials. That way, if you do make a mistake, you will have a reserve board to bail you out. Returning to the store for just one more board is frustrating, time-consuming, and (depending upon how far you drive) sometimes more expensive than if you had purchased an extra one on the original trip.

FINISHES

There is no need to apply a finish to treated lumber. But coatings add additional protection to wood and can enhance the appearance of the finished furniture. Because different finishes will have some effect on the material you use, you need to decide on the type of finish you want to apply *before* you buy the lumber. For instance, if you plan to stain the finished piece, pay particular attention to the grain of the wood that you are buying, and choose boards that have few imperfections and similar grain patterns. If you are going to paint the finished piece, you can purchase a lower grade of wood, and cover the defects with wood filler and paint after the piece is built.

It goes without saying that every finish used on outdoor projects must be rated for exterior use. There are hundreds of different products on the market, but the first choice is whether to seal, stain, or paint your project.

Sealer The finish that will affect the wood's appearance the least is a clear wood finish, often referred to as a water sealer. It is most commonly used on decks and railings. Clear wood finish is available as an oil-based or as a waterborne product. Its actual appearance can range from a muted, almost invisible finish to a smooth semi-gloss sheen. Make sure you buy a finish sealer, not a clear sanding sealer, which is used under paints and stains to prime the wood. You can apply a wood finish sealer with a brush or roller or you can spray it on.

Stain Stains used to come in brown (or brown). True, there were gray-browns and yellow-browns and red-browns—but they were all brown. And it used to be very difficult to apply them evenly. How times have changed! These days stains come in a terrific variety of colors—from the palest white to the darkest black. They also range from extremely translucent to nearly opaque. Stains have the additional advantage of being extremely easy to apply, and usually require only one coat. Although most manufacturers recommend that you apply their product with a brush, I have found that a plain old rag gives a very smooth and even appearance to most stains. (This may not give the best results with every type of stain, so, before attacking the entire project with my method, try it on a scrap of wood or on a surface that will not show.)

Paint Paint will cover a multitude of flaws. It is possible to take wood that is not at all attractive in appearance, apply a flawless coat of paint, and produce an extremely good-looking piece of furniture. The disadvantage to using paint on a piece of 2 x 4 furniture is that the wood must be thoroughly filled, sanded, and primed—all of which takes time and effort. Then the wood must be given two coats of paint, and at least one coat of sealer should be applied after the paint has dried.

When shopping for paint, look for special characteristics that protect wood against local weather problems. Here in Florida, many paints are treated with special additives that protect against mildew, which occurs in our high humidity. Also check to see how long the paint is warranted.

Brushes Most professionals swear by very expensive hog-bristle brushes. We use them only when there is absolutely no choice in the matter. We much prefer sponge brushes, which are extremely cheap and can be thrown in the trash after use. Look for the ones that have a smooth surface like a cosmetic sponge and a wooden handle. If you are interrupted in midcoat, and the sponge brush is not yet ready for tossing, just pop your brush into an airtight sandwich bag. You can leave it there for a day or so, and it will still be pliable and ready to use.

The finish that you apply to your completed project is extremely important when building

anything that will be used outdoors. Your choice of finish, and the care with which you apply it, will make a considerable difference in the weather resistance of the furniture. The better the finish, the longer you will be enjoying your handiwork. No matter how you finish your furniture, we recommend that you cover or store it when it is not in use.

FASTENERS

The projects in this book are designed for exterior use, so any fastener you use to construct them must also be weatherproof—or at least weather resistant. There are several different kinds of materials and coatings that make a nail or screw suitable for exterior use. The basic rule is that the longer the coating or material is expected to last, the more you can expect to pay for it.

The most popular choices for nails and screws used for outdoor woodworking are described below.

Galvanized: Coated with zinc, inexpensive, and the most widely used type of coating. Over

time, may stain redwood and cedar, and corrode in pressure-treated wood.

Anodized: Roughly equivalent to galvanized

Zinc-plated: Somewhat more weather resistant, but difficult to find outside specialty stores

Brass: Lovely to look at, resistant to weather, but lacks strength

Stainless steel: Highly resistant to corrosion, extremely strong, but extremely expensive

Here is one more note about galvanizing: It may be worth the extra trouble to look for what are known as "hot-dipped" or mechanically galvanized nails or screws rather than the somewhat less expensive products that use an electrical plating technique. The dipping process more effectively deposits zinc on the surface of the metal.

Ultimately, we tend to match the quality of the fasteners we choose to the quality of the wood. For example, if you are building a project out of expensive teak, it makes sense to purchase stainless steel screws. If you are using inexpensive pressure-treated pine, galvanized decking screws are probably the logical choice.

Nails Although there are many different types of nails (common, large flathead, duplex head, oval head, etc.), the one most commonly used in woodworking is a finishing nail. It has a much smaller head than the common nail, making it easy to recess below the surface of the wood (*countersinking* the nail). The small hole remaining on the surface is easily concealed with wood filler.

Nail sizes are designated by "penny" (abbreviated as "d"). Penny size directly corresponds to length, although the diameter is larger for longer nails. Nails range in length from 1 inch to 6 inches. Confused? To determine the penny size of a particular nail length, the following method works well for lengths up to

three inches (10d). Take the length of the nail you need, subtract ½ inch, and multiply by 4. For example, if you need a 2½-inch nail, subtract ½ inch, and multiply by 4. What you need is an 8-penny nail (8d). Some of the more commonly used sizes of nails are listed in the table below.

Penny Size	Length (Inches)
2d	1
3d	1¼
4d	1½
5d	1¾
6d	2
7d	2¼
8d	2½
9d	2¾
10d	3
12d	3¼
16d	3½
20d	4

Working with Nails As a general rule, when joining two pieces of wood together, use a nail length that will provide the greatest amount of holding power without penetrating the opposite surface. For example, if you are joining two 1 x 4s, each piece of wood is ¾ inches thick—a total of 1½ inches of wood. To maximize your holding power, you should choose a 1¼-inch-long nail.

Nails driven in at an angle provide more holding power than those that are driven straight into the work. *Toenailing* refers to the process of driving a nail into the wood at an extreme angle to secure two pieces together. The most difficult part of toenailing comes when the nail is nearly all the way in the wood and only the head and a bit of the shank are visible. To avoid making hammer marks on your wood, hammer the nail into the piece until the head is still slightly above the surface. Then use a nail set to finish the job and countersink the nail.

In fact, the best way to prevent hammer marks on all of your work is to use a nail set. The trick to using a nail set effectively is to hold it in the proper manner. It should be steadied with the hand by gripping it firmly with all four fingers and your thumb. Rest your little finger on the surface of the wood for added stability.

If you are working with hardwood, a very narrow piece of softwood, or any wood that has a tendency to split when you nail into it, you may want to predrill the nail hole. Choose a drill bit that is just barely smaller than the diameter of the nail, and drill a pilot hole about two-thirds the length of the nail.

Brads Wire brads are used for attaching trim or for very small projects. They are just a smaller and thinner version of finishing nails. Brads are designated in length in inches and wire gauge numbers from 11 to 20. The lower the gauge number, the larger the diameter.

Staples and Staple Guns Staples are another light-duty fastener, often used to attach fabric to wood. A staple gun is a

TOENAILING

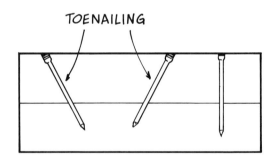

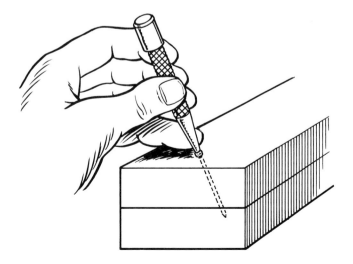

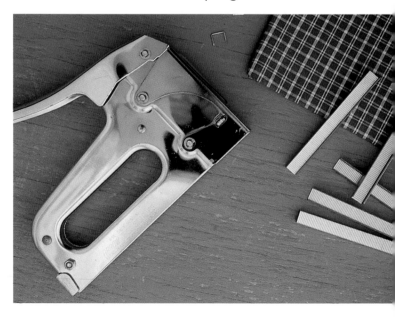

worthwhile investment and a handy piece of equipment to have around the house. Staple guns are available in many sizes and prices, and, although electric models are available and nice to have, a heavy-duty hand staple gun will probably be all that you need initially. It is worthwhile to purchase staples in a variety of lengths to have them on hand to accommodate different thicknesses of materials.

Screws The advantage of screws over nails is their holding power, and the fact that, when used without glue, they can be removed easily at a later date. Their disadvantage is that they are not as easy to insert.

As with nails, there are many kinds of screws. The one most often used in woodworking is a flathead Phillips screw. As the name implies, it has a flat head that can be countersunk below the surface. The Phillips screw can be driven with a power drill. Regular straight-slotted, flathead screws work, too, but they take more time to install because they require a pilot hole and don't do as well with power screwdrivers.

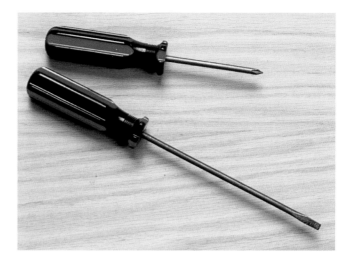

Screws are designated by length and diameter. In general, as with nails, you want to use the longest screw possible that won't penetrate the opposite surface, with a thickness that won't split the board. The diameter of a screw is described by its gauge number. Common sizes are listed below.

Screw Chart

Size or gauge no.	4	6	8	10	12
Shank diameter	7/64"	9/64"	5/32"	3/16"	7/32"
Lengths (by 1/4's)	3/8"-1	1/2"-2"	1/2"-3"	3/4"-31/2"	3/4-31/2"

To assemble all the projects in this book, we used galvanized decking screws with Phillips-head slots. They are easy to drive into wood with a hand or power screwdriver, are inexpensive, and last a long time without corroding. You can also use more expensive zinc-plated or stainless steel wood screws.

Working with Screws When you are working on very soft wood, it is possible to countersink a screw simply by driving it with a power drill. However, the resulting surface hole may be covered only by using wood filler. An alternate method is to predrill the screw hole and insert a wood plug over the top of the countersunk screw head.

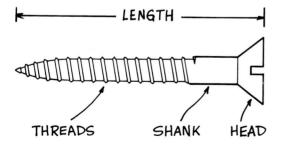

LENGTH

THREADS   SHANK   HEAD

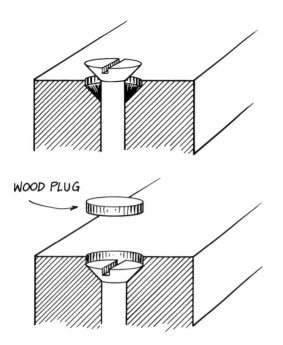

WOOD PLUG

This predrilling is normally a two-step operation. First drill the pilot hole using a drill bit the same diameter as the solid portion of the screw (minus the threads). Then drill the larger, countersunk portion deep enough and at a diameter just slightly larger than the diameter of the screw head (or the depth and diameter needed to accommodate the screw and the wood plug you are using). The larger-diameter countersunk portion of the drilling will center itself over the pilot hole. If you use the same size screws on a

regular basis, you may wish to invest in a combination pilot-countersink bit for your drill, which will perform both operations at the same time.

You can purchase wood plugs or you can cut your own. It is easy to slice a wooden dowel rod into many wood plugs. The only disadvantage to this plug is that it will show the end grain, and will be visible if you stain the wood. The alternative is to cut your own plugs using a plug cutter.

Screws can be inserted at an angle, the same way that nails are, to toenail two pieces of wood together. After some practice, you will be able to start a screw at any angle with very little or no effort. If you find it difficult, simply use a drill or a screw starter to begin your screw hole.

Although you don't want to add so many screws to your project that the metal outweighs the wood, we are not stingy with them. If there is the slightest chance that the joint could be shaky, we added a couple of extra screws. Remember that the project you are making probably will be subjected to several moves over the course of the years—either to a different room or a different house—which will place additional strain on the joints.

ADHESIVES

Since this book deals with exterior projects, a weatherproof glue is mandatory. Ordinary interior glue will dissolve when exposed to the elements. The easiest glue to use is an exterior-formulated version of ordinary straw-colored carpenter's glue. Look for the words "exterior use" on the container. If this type of adhesive is not available, you may use the more costly two-part resorcinol, though it takes about 12 hours to set and at least another 12 to cure completely.

Don't overdo the amount of glue. If too much is applied, the glue will be squeezed out of the joint and drip all over your project when pressure is applied. Just apply a small ribbon of glue down the center of one surface and then rub the adjoining surface against the ribbon to distribute the glue evenly. Your objective is to coat both surfaces with a uniform, thin coating. If you do encounter drips, wipe them off quickly with a damp cloth. It is easy to do at the moment, but if you let the glue dry, it is difficult to remove. If the glue drip does dry, it will have to be sanded off, since it will not accept most stains.

TOOLS

If you are just beginning in woodworking, you may have the mistaken idea that it costs thousands of dollars to be involved in woodworking. Not true! Unless they are independently wealthy, most woodworkers start with a few hand tools, and over time add portable power tools to their workshop. Obviously, there weren't too many power tools when Louis XV's furniture craftsmen were at work—all of history's magnificent furniture was built using only hand tools. The obvious reason for power tools is that they get the job done faster.

Our goal is to create a good-looking piece of furniture in the least amount of time. So over the years we have added power tools that cut the time required to complete the job and require a lot less physical effort. We use a power drill rather than a manual drill and a circular saw rather than a handsaw. A good approach is to add a tool to your workshop each time that you build a large project. By building the piece of furniture, rather than buying it, you will have saved a substantial amount of money, and you will have the tool for the next project.

Probably, many of you own a few portable power tools, such as a circular saw and a power drill. But even if you have only a handsaw and a screwdriver, you can make some of the projects in this book. Some tools are needed for every project, but others are required only for a few pieces. You may want to choose your first project according to the tools you have available. To determine which tools you will need, read through the instructions before starting a project.

If you are starting from scratch, buy the best tools that you can afford. A bargain screwdriver that falls apart after inserting three screws is not much of a bargain, and the resulting frustration is not worth the two-dollar savings. Look for the manufacturer's warranty when purchasing tools. If they offer a lifetime guarantee, it's a safe bet that it's a good tool.

As with most hobbies, when you purchase your equipment, you should consider your physical size and ability. A golf club or a tennis racquet must be matched to the person using it. In the same way, a physically large person may be able to use a very large hammer. While it is true that the larger hammer will drive the nail into the wood faster, it doesn't mean very much if you are able to swing a heavier hammer only twice before you feel your arm going weak from the strain. So—try before you buy! Lift the tool a number of times before you decide that it is for you. The same philosophy applies to portable power tools. It requires a great deal of strength to control a 4-inch-wide belt sander, but almost anyone can use a 2-inch-wide sander.

A hammer and saw probably come to mind when someone discusses woodworking. However, other tools are just as important. A solid work surface, a ready supply of clamps, and the right sanding equipment can make woodworking an enjoyable pursuit; the lack of them can spell complete frustration.

WORK SURFACE

Although most people would not put it at the top of the list, one of the most important tools in woodworking is a work surface that is smooth and level. If you construct a project on an uneven work surface, chances are that your table legs will be uneven or the cabinet top will slope downhill. Your work surface doesn't have to be a professional-quality mahogany workbench—it just has to be level and even. It can be as simple as an old door (flush, not paneled) or a piece of thick plywood supported by sawhorses.

To level your work surface, simply set a fairly long level in various places on the surface, and turn it so that it faces in several directions. Then shim the surfaces with thicknesses of wood to lift the surface until it is perfectly level. Be sure to attach the shim with glue and nails or screws to make certain that it stays in place while you work.

CLAMPS

Clamps are an absolute must for woodworking. They are used to apply pressure and hold joints together until the glue sets, and they are valuable aids when assembling a project. A single person can assemble a large project by using clamps—a job that otherwise requires the concerted effort of two or more people. When you buy clamps, it is advisable to get two clamps of the same type. This is because you almost always use them in pairs to provide even pressure on the work.

When you apply clamps, always insert a scrap of wood between the clamp and your work to act as a cushion. That way you will avoid leaving clamp marks on the surface of your project.

There have been some fairly recent improvements in woodworking clamps. A new type looks like a regular bar clamp, but instead of a screw mechanism to tighten it, this clamp has a trigger much like a caulk gun. This makes the clamp especially useful because it can be operated with one hand. It also has a quick-release mechanism. I recommend this kind of clamp for a beginner, since it is easy to use, works well, and comes in a variety of lengths.

Old-fashioned wood clamps are a nice addition

to your workshop, too. They are extremely versatile since they can be adjusted to clamp offsetting surfaces.

"C" clamps are inexpensive and useful for many woodworking applications. One end of their C-shaped frame is fixed; the other end is fitted with a threaded rod and swivel pad that can be clamped tightly across an opening, ranging from zero to several inches or more, depending upon the size of the clamp. They can hold two thicknesses of wood together, secure a piece of wood to a work surface, and perform many other functions.

Bar clamps and pipe clamps can be used to hold assemblies together temporarily while you add the fasteners, as well as to apply pressure to laminates. While they look very much alike and function the same way, pipe clamps are significantly less expensive than bar clamps. You buy the fittings separately, and they can be used with various lengths of pipe, depending upon

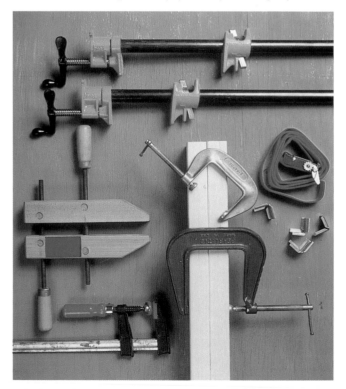

Clockwise from top: pipe clamps, web clamp (band clamp), C clamps (middle), bar clamp, wood hand clamp

the need. You can also buy rubber "shoes" that fit over the pipe clamp fittings, which will eliminate clamp marks on the wood.

Web clamps (or band clamps) are used for clamping such things as chairs or drawers, where a uniform pressure needs to be exerted completely around a project. The clamp consists of a continuous band with an attached metal mechanism that can be ratcheted to pull the band tightly around the object.

MEASURING

If you have been involved with woodworking at all, you have probably heard the expression "measure twice—cut once." And it is always worth repeating. If you measure accurately and cut carefully to that measurement, your project will fit together perfectly during final assembly. Accurate cutting depends on accurate measurements. So a quality measuring tool is a sound investment. A wide steel tape rule is a good choice for most projects. A narrow tape will bend more easily along the length of a board and will be less accurate. Consistently use the

Clockwise from top right corner: level, straightedge, tape measure, combination square, sliding T-bevel

CHART: Basic Tools

- Working surface that is smooth and level
- Measuring tools: tape measure, level, combination square
- Hammers: two hammers (large and small), tack hammer, nail set
- Screwdrivers (hand and/or power): assortment of flathead and Phillips sizes
- Saws: combination saw, or ripsaw and crosscut saw; saber saw, circular saw, selection of blades
- Drill: hand or power drill and a variety of bits
- Clamps: Two "quick clamps," two wood hand clamps
- Sanding tools: sanding block and assortment of sandpaper from fine to coarse

Optional Tools:

- Measuring tools: framing square
- Clamps: two "C" clamps, web clamp, two bar clamps
- Chisels: ¼-inch, ¾-inch, and 1-inch wide
- Finishing sander
- Router
- Safety equipment: goggles, dust mask (use with power tools)

Advanced Tools (Nice to have):

- Belt sander
- Table saw
- Band saw
- Drill press

same measuring device throughout the cutting process. Unless you have precise measuring tools, any two instruments may vary enough to give you slightly different measurements.

A straightedge (an ordinary steel ruler, 12 to 24 inches long) is a handy woodworking tool for quick measurements.

A sliding T-bevel is valuable for establishing bevel angles. The steel blade pivots and slides within a handle, and can be locked in position to form an angle. It is used to check and transfer bevels and mitered ends.

Squares are versatile and essential tools in woodworking. The most commonly used types are the framing square (or carpenter's square)

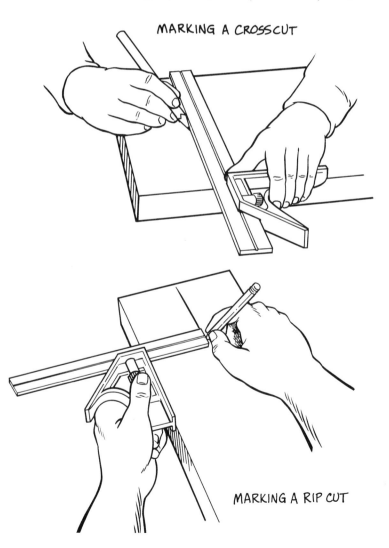

MARKING A CROSSCUT

MARKING A RIP CUT

and the combination square. In addition to their obvious use for marking a cutting line on a board and obtaining a right angle, squares can be used to check the outer or inner squareness of a joint, to guide a saw through a cut, and much more.

TECHNIQUES

CUTTING

For purposes of clarity, this book refers to each surface of a board by a specific name. The broadest part of the board is called a *face*, and the narrow surface along the length of the board is an edge. The *ends*, as the name suggests, are the smallest surfaces occurring on the extremities of each board.

Keep in mind that every saw blade has a thickness, called a *kerf*, that is removed from the wood when you cut. (From whence cometh the gigantic amount of sawdust that accumulates when you make a project.) When you measure and mark a board, measure precisely. When you cut the board at your mark, set the saw so that the blade will *exactly* remove the mark. Cut so that you also remove the mark from the end of the board that will be waste.

A piece of wood may be either *ripped* (cut along the length of the board) or *crosscut* (cut across the width of the board). There are specific hand tools for each procedure. A rip saw has teeth designed for cutting along the length of the board, with the grain. It comes with 4½ through 7 points per inch, the latter being the smoothest cut. The crosscut saw is made to cut across the grain. Crosscut saws are available with 7 through 12 points per inch, depending on how coarse or fine you wish to the cut be. The greater the number, the smoother the cut.

Probably the most popular power cutting tool is the circular saw. The blade can be adjusted to cut at a 90-degree or 45-degree angle, or any angle in between.

While saw blades for power tools are also designed for ripping and crosscutting, the most practical blade for general woodworking is a combination blade. It rips and crosscuts with equal ease. Carbide-tipped blades are more expensive, but well worth the cost since they last much longer than regular blades.

The hand-held jigsaw or saber saw is used to cut curves, shapes, and large holes in panels or boards up to 1½ inches in thickness. Its cutting action comes from a narrow reciprocating "bayonet" blade that moves up and down very quickly. The best saber saws have a variable speed control and an orbital blade action which swings the cutting edge forward into the work and back again during the blade's up-and-down cycle. A dust blower keeps the sawdust away from the cut.

When you are cutting either lumber or plywood, note the type of cut that your tool is making, and use it to your advantage. For example, circular saws and saber saws cut on the upstroke, so they may leave ragged edges on the upper surface of your wood. When using these saws, you should position the wood with the better surface facing down when cutting.

Clockwise from top corner: handsaw, hand-held jigsaw, plane, circular saw, chisels (middle)

Certain types of cuts, such as hollowing out a section of wood, are done with chisels. Using a chisel well takes some practice, but it is worth the effort because chisels can perform unique woodworking tasks. Always work with sharp chisels. For your first purchase, choose two different sizes—one very narrow and one about an inch wide.

WOOD JOINTS

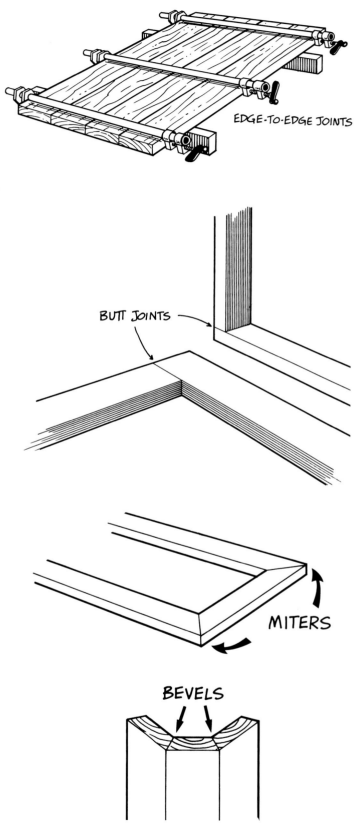

EDGE-TO-EDGE JOINTS

BUTT JOINTS

MITERS

BEVELS

There are hundreds of different kinds of wood joints. They range in complexity from the plainest butt joint to incredibly intricate and time-consuming ones. The projects in this book are constructed with only the simplest joints, secured with glue, and fastened with either nails or screws, or both.

Edge-to-edge joint: This joint is used when laminating boards together edge to edge to obtain a wider piece of wood. To ensure a perfect meeting between boards, a minuscule amount should be ripped from each edge of each board. Then apply glue to the adjoining edges and clamp the boards together.

Apply even pressure along the length of the piece. The boards should be firmly clamped, but not so tightly that all of the glue is forced out, or that the lamination starts to bow across its width. On a long lamination, extra boards may be placed above and below the lamination, across the width, and those boards clamped with "C" clamps or wood clamps. Wipe off any excess glue that is squeezed out in the clamping process.

Butt joint: This is the simplest of joints, where one board abuts another at a right angle. This method offers the least holding power of any joint. It must be reinforced with some kind of fastener, usually screws.

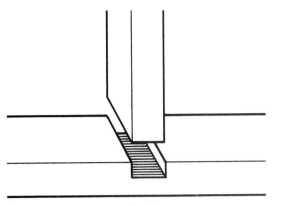

DADO

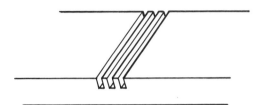

CUT DADO TO DEPTH WITH SAW

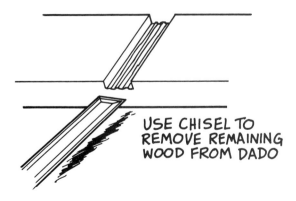

USE CHISEL TO REMOVE REMAINING WOOD FROM DADO

Miter: A miter is a angle cut across the width of a board. It is used to joint two pieces of wood without exposing the end grain of either piece. A mitered joint must also be reinforced with nails or screws. The angle most often cut is 45 degrees, which is used to construct a right angle when two mitered boards are joined together.

Bevel: A bevel is also an angular cut, but it refers to an angle cut along the length of a board, rather than across the width as in a miter.

Dado: A dado is a groove cut in the face of one board to accommodate the thickness of another board. It can be cut with a hand saw and chisel, with a router, or with a dado set on a table saw.

No matter what kind of joint you are making, it is advisable to use both glue and fasteners (nails or screws) whenever possible. The only exception, when you may want to omit the glue, is on joints that you wish to disassemble at a later time.

Particularly if you are a beginner, you may wish to dry-fit your project. This means that you can preassemble portions of the project without glue to make certain that all of the pieces were cut correctly and fit together tightly. You can use clamps to hold the pieces together temporarily, or simply hammer small nails into the surface just far enough to hold them in place. Leave a large portion of the nail head above the surface, so it is easy to remove at a later date. Check the fit, and trim or adjust the pieces as necessary. Then remove the clamps and/or nails, apply glue, and reassemble the pieces.

SANDING

Of course, any project may be sanded by hand. An inexpensive plastic sanding block will do the job of sanding a level surface just fine. You can even wrap a block of wood with a piece of sandpaper. If you need to sand moldings or curves, try wrapping a pencil or other appropriate-sized object with sandpaper.

The amount of sanding that you do on each project depends in a large part on the intended use of the project, and on what kind of finish you plan to use. Obviously, if you prefer a rustic look for your project, it need not be sanded completely smooth. However, a rustic chair requires more sanding than a rustic table— someone will be sitting on it. An orbital sander does a good job of beginning the sanding process, but it may leave circular marks that must be subsequently sanded out by hand.

A finishing sander is probably the most practical power sander for furniture projects. It has the ability to smooth the surface quickly, and it does not leave circular marks.

A belt sander is often used for large jobs. It sands quickly, but it is difficult to control on softwood such as pine. Because of its power, a belt sander can easily gouge softwood, or if you don't watch carefully, it can remove more of the wood than you wish.

No matter what tool you use, begin sanding with coarse grit and gradually progress to sandpaper with a fine grit.

SAFETY

Working with power tools can be dangerous. In a tie with a power saw, you will be the loser. And losing is extremely painful. I know many woodworkers, and many of them have missing digits. If that sounds scary, that's good. Read the instructions that are provided with every tool and follow them religiously.

Again, we stress that the instructions in this book are written for the beginner using hand tools and basic portable power tools, and must be altered when using stationary power tools to accommodate the requirements of those

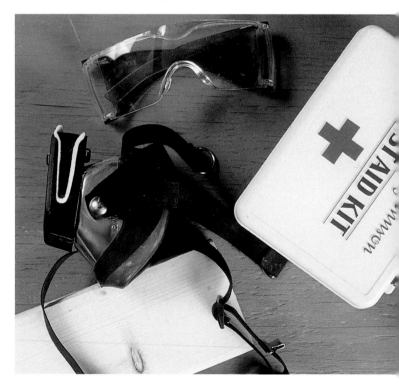

advanced tools. Never attempt any woodworking maneuver that does not translate to power tools. Misuse of power tool equipment can lead to serious injury to yourself or damage to the tool.

Never take your eyes off the work: always concentrate on what you are doing, and take the necessary safety precautions. Just one moment of lost concentration or not following the safety rules can result in frightful consequences. Develop the habit of avoiding the path of the saw: do not stand directly behind it or directly in front of it. Power saws can flip a piece of wood back at you with incredible force.

Always wear safety goggles when working with wood. Avoiding just one splinter aimed at your eye makes this practice worth your while. A dust mask is also a prudent accessory when working with wood. Sawdust can be very irritating to your lungs. You can choose from a number of different masks, from a simple paper mask to those with replaceable filters.

If you use power tools for extended periods— especially a power saw, which can be quite loud—a pair of ear plugs or protectors is a good investment. Prolonged exposure to loud noise can have harmful effects on your hearing.

Practicing all of these safety rules will keep you safe and make woodworking a pleasure.

THE PROJECTS

Every project in this book includes lists of the materials, supplies, and hardware you need to build that project. Although we haven't listed every tool and every woodworking technique used, we do identify special tools and techniques required for certain projects. It's always a good idea to read the project lists and all the instructions at least once before deciding what project to undertake. That way, you'll know right away what to expect.

SKILL LEVEL

This is a book designed for beginning woodworkers, although experienced woodworkers will enjoy building the projects, too. If we didn't think someone new to woodworking could handle all the projects, we wouldn't have included all of them in the book. But some of the projects demand more time, patience, and technique to accomplish than others. As is true of other skills, woodworking skills are developed with practice. We suggest that you begin by constructing one or two of the quick-to-build projects, such as the plant pedestal, footstool, or hurricane lamp. You will soon acquire the necessary skills and confidence to tackle projects that are more challenging.

SPECIAL TOOLS AND TECHNIQUES

This list lets you know that special tools and techniques are required, tools you may not own and skills you may not have. If you read "mitering" in this list and you've never cut a miter, look up miters in the index on page 128, and read the appropriate section. Then, take the time to practice cutting a few miters on scrap wood. Before you know it, you'll have the confidence to tackle miters and to successfully build that table or bench.

MATERIALS AND SUPPLIES

This list identifies in linear feet the total amount of lumber you'll need to purchase. Softwood, such as pine, is sold in standard dimensional sizes, such as 2 x 4 and 1 x 2, and in specific lengths, such as 6-foot, 8-foot, etc. The bin labeled 2 x 4 x 8 at your local building-supply outlet contains 2 x 4 boards that are 8 feet long. If the Materials and Supplies list specifies 23

linear feet of 1 x 4 pine, you can buy two 1 x 4s, each 12 feet long, or four 1 x 4s, each 6 feet long. It's important to read through the Cutting List and the instructions before deciding what lengths to buy.

CUTTING LIST

This list specifies the exact size of each piece of wood you'll need to cut from the lumber. Reviewing the linear feet quantities and the Cutting List information will tell you what lengths of a particular wood to purchase. You'll come up short if you buy all of your 1 x 4s in 6-foot lengths, and then discover that your project requires two pieces, each 7 feet long. When you get to the lumber outlet, carefully inspect the various lengths available. If you find that the 8-foot 2 x 4s are knotted and warped, while the 6-foot and 10-foot lengths are nearly perfect, it would make sense to purchase the required total linear feet in these boards.

It's a good idea to purchase 10 to 20 percent more lumber than you need. Having to return to the store to buy one more 2 x 4 because you miscut a board is far more expensive in terms of time and energy than a few extra feet of lumber. Remember, too, that the ends of boards aren't always square, so you need to allow for having to square them before you begin measuring. You can always use the leftover wood when you build the next project.

Don't cut the pieces of wood to size right away; the instructions will walk you through cutting each piece.

ONE FINAL NOTE

All experienced woodworkers have their share of miscut boards, misdrilled holes, and mishaps with hammers landing on thumbs. If any of these missteps happen to you, it's probably time to take a break. The best safeguard against woodworking accidents, both minor and major, is a patient, content, and attentive mind. So when you start to make mistakes, go for a walk, take a nap, eat an apple—and then resume building.

ADIRONDACK CHAIR

Our own version of this furniture classic retains its essential characteristics: it's a perfect place to sit and enjoy a summer evening. The chair is equally at home in a garden, on a front porch, or on a boat dock. We originally planned to build just one chair, but quickly decided that one was just not enough. The chairs have become our family favorites.

Special Tools and Techniques

C-clamp

Bar clamp (optional)

Materials and Supplies (for one chair)

17 linear feet of 1 x 6 pine

28 linear feet of 1 x 4 pine

4 linear feet of 1 x 2 pine

3 linear feet of 2 x 4 pine

Hardware

50 3d x 1-¼" nails

60 1¼" screws

4 carriage bolts, ⅜ " x 2" with washer and nut

2 carriage bolts, ⅜" x 3" with washer and nut

Cutting List

Code	Description	Qty.	Materials	Dimensions
A	Seat Brace	2	1 x 6 pine	39" long
B	Front Seat Trim	1	1 x 6 pine	22" long
C	Seat Side	2	1 x 4 pine	24" long
D	Seat Slat	6	1 x 4 pine	22" long
E	Short Back Slat	2	1 x 4 pine	28" long
F	Medium Back Slat	2	1 x 4 pine	30" long
G	Long Back Slat	1	1 x 6 pine	32" long
H	Back Support	2	1 x 2 pine	22" long
I	Arm	2	1 x 6 pine	27" long
J	Arm Connector	1	2 x 4 pine	28½" long
K	Arm Brace	2	1 x 4 pine	9" long

Making the Seat

1. The trademark of the Adirondack chair is the angled seat. The braces that support the seat are simple to construct, but require exact dimensions to work. Cut two seat braces (A) from 1 x 6 pine, each measuring 39 inches long.

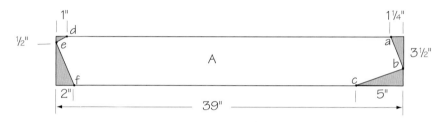

Figure 1

To achieve the necessary angles for the seat braces (A), refer to figure 1. Portions of the seat braces must be cut away. This is as simple as "connect the letters." Following the measurements in figure 1, label each point, and draw a straight line from "a" to "b," "b" to "c," "d" to "e," and "e" to "f". Cut along the lines you have just drawn to eliminate the shaded portions of one seat brace (A), as shown in figure 1. Use the resulting seat brace (A) as a pattern to cut the other seat brace (A).

2. Cut one front seat trim (B) from 1 x 6 pine, measuring 22 inches long.

3. The front seat trim (B) will be used to connect the two seat braces (A). Position the two seat braces parallel to each other and on edge, with the "e-f" edge facing up, 20½ inches apart.

Fit the seat trim (B) over the "e-f" edges, as shown in figure 2. Nail through the front seat trim (B) into the ends of the seat braces (A) using three 1¼-inch-long nails on each joint.

4. Cut two seat sides (C) from 1 x 4 pine, each measuring 24 inches long.

5. Turn the assembly right side up. Follow figure 3 to connect the seat sides (C) to the seat braces (A), attaching them 6 inches from the top edge of the seat sides (C) and flush with the seat trim (B) on the front. Use two 2-inch-long carriage bolts to secure each of the joints, spacing them about 3 inches apart.

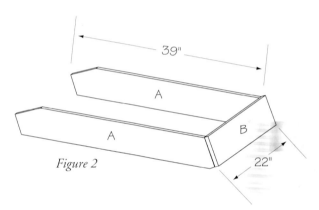

Figure 2

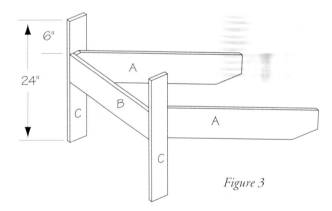

Figure 3

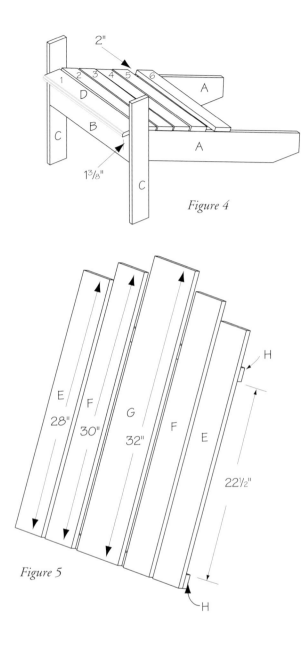

Figure 4

Figure 5

Adding the Seat Slats

6. Cut six seat slats (D) from 1 x 4 pine, each measuring 22 inches long.

7. For comfort, round off the long edge of the slat (D) that will be attached to the front of the chair. Attach this slat to the "d-e" edges of the seat braces (A) so that it extends 1⅜ inches over the seat trim (B), as shown in figure 4. Use two 1¼-inch-long nails on each side, and four nails spaced evenly across the front.

8. Attach the next four seat slats (D) to the seat braces (A), as shown in figure 4, spacing them approximately ⅜ inch apart. Use two 1¼-inch-long nails on each joint. Attach the sixth slat (D) 2 inches from the fifth seat slat (D). This space will be needed later to accommodate the back of the chair.

Constructing the Back

9. Cut two short back slats (E) from 1 x 4 pine, each measuring 28 inches long.

10. Cut two medium back slats (F) from 1 x 4 pine, each measuring 30 inches long.

11. Cut one long back slat (G) from 1 x 6 pine, measuring 32 inches long.

12. Cut two back supports (H) from 1 x 2 pine, each measuring 22 inches long.

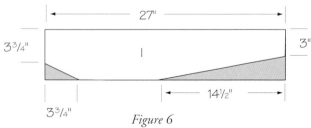

Figure 6

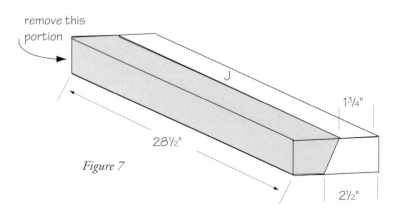

Figure 7

13. Place the two back supports (H) on a level surface, parallel to each other and 22½ inches apart.

14. Place the five back slats (E, F, and G) on top of the two back supports (H), spaced evenly, approximately ½ inch apart, as shown in figure 5 on page 34. Place the two short back slats (E) on the outside, the two medium back slats (F) in the middle, and the long back slat (G) in the center. Make sure that the back slats are square to the back supports (H). Note that the ends of all of the back slats (E, F, and G) are even with one back support (H) at what will be the lower chair back, and the opposite ends of the back slats are at various lengths at what will be the top of the chair back. Screw through each of the back slats (E, F, and G) into each of the back supports (H). Use two 1¼-inch-long screws at each joint.

Constructing the Arm Assembly

15. Cut two arms (I) from 1 x 6 pine, each measuring 27 inches long.

16. Follow the diagram shown in figure 6 on page 34 to remove the shaded portions from one arm (I) in the same manner you used to cut

the seat braces (step 1, page 30). Use this cut arm as a pattern to cut the other arm (I).

17. Cut one arm connector (J) from 2 x 4 pine, measuring 28½ inches long.

18. In order to accommodate the back of the chair, one edge of the arm connector (J) must be angled. Rip the arm connector (J) 20 degrees along its length, as shown in figure 7 on page 34.

19. Place the two arms (I) over the ends of the arm connector (J). Make certain that the space between the two arms (J) is just slightly over 22 inches in order to accommodate the back assembly. Clamp the two arms (I) to the ends of the arm connector (J).

Final Assembly

20. Although you can perform this assembly with the assistance of bar clamps, it's easier to enlist the aid of a helper. First, fit the back assembly into the 2-inch-wide gap in the seat slats, with the back slats facing the front of the chair, as shown in figure 8. Then wrap the

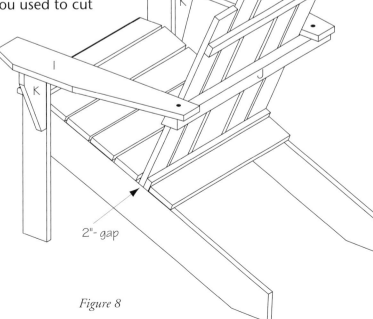

Figure 8

2"- gap

clamped arm assembly around the back of the chair so that the front of the arm rests on the chair sides. Have the helper sit in the chair; then adjust the clamped arm assembly so that the arms are level to the floor and the back of the chair is at the most comfortable angle. Screw through the arms (I) to secure them to the chair sides, using two 1¼-inch-long screws on each joint. Mark the placement of the arm connector on the back assembly. (Remove the helper!)

21. Screw through each of the back slats (E, F, and G) into the arm connector (J). Use two 1¼-inch-long screws on each of the joints.

22. Drill a ⅜"-wide hole in each arm (I) through the arm connector (J), and secure the joint by inserting a 3-inch-long carriage bolt through the drilled holes. Add a washer and a nut, and tighten the bolt securely.

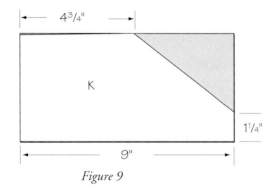

Figure 9

23. Cut two arm braces (K) from 1 x 4 pine, each measuring 9 inches long. Follow the diagram in figure 9 to remove the shaded portion of one of the arm braces. Use the resulting piece as a pattern to mark and cut the second arm brace.

24. Fit the arm braces (K) onto the seat sides (C), under the arms, with the 9-inch-long edge facing the seat sides (C), as shown in figure 8 on page 35. Screw through the seat sides (C) and arms (I) into the arm braces (K) using two or three 1¼-inch-long screws on each joint.

Finishing

25. Fill any screw holes with wood filler. Sand all surfaces thoroughly. Remember that people will be sitting on this project, so don't spare the sandpaper! No one likes splinters in the derriere!

26. We primed and painted our Adirondack chair, but you can let it weather naturally, or stain it the color of your choice.

FOOTSTOOL

This simple footstool has been put to many uses in our backyard. We have used it to accompany our Garden Sofa (page 51) and our Adirondack Chair (page 30). Great as a footrest, it also provides a handy surface for a stack of magazines or a pitcher of iced tea. And if things get crowded, this nifty footstool can double as an extra seat.

Materials and Supplies

11 linear feet of 2 x 4 pine
14 linear feet of 1 x 4 pine

Hardware

10   2½" screws
15   3d x 1¼" nails

Cutting List

Code	Description	Qty.	Materials	Dimensions
A	Long Horizontal	2	2 x 4 pine	21" long
B	Leg	4	2 x 4 pine	12" long
C	Short Horizontal	2	2 x 4 pine	13" long
D	Slat	8	1 x 4 pine	18" long

Constructing the Base

1. Cut two long horizontals (A) from 2 x 4 pine, each measuring 21 inches long.

2. Cut four legs (B) from 2 x 4 pine, each measuring 12 inches long.

3. Place two legs (B) on a level surface, parallel to each other and 20 inches apart. Fit one long horizontal (A) between the two legs (B), flush with the ends of the legs (B), as shown in figure 1. Toenail through the ends of the long horizontals (A) into the legs (B). Use two 2½-inch-long screws on each joint.

4. Repeat step 3 to attach the remaining long horizontal (A) to the other two legs (B).

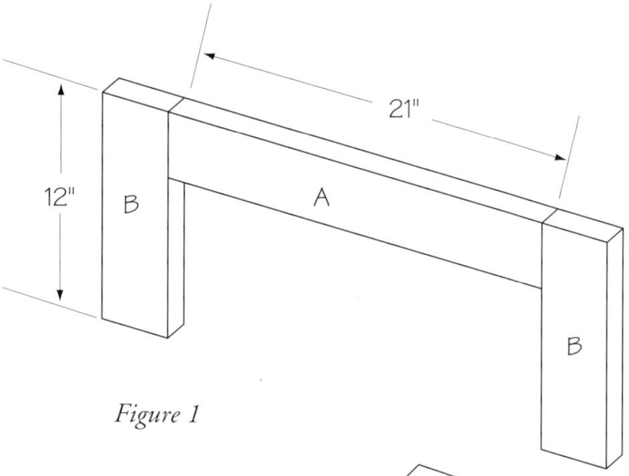

Figure 1

5. Cut two short horizontals (C) from 2 x 4 pine, each measuring 13 inches long.

6. Place the two leg assemblies upside down on a level surface, parallel to each other and 13 inches apart, as shown in figure 2. Fit the short horizontals (C) between the two leg assemblies, flush with the outer legs (B). Screw through the legs (B) into the ends of the short horizontals. Use two 2½-inch-long screws on each joint.

Adding the Slats

7. Cut eight slats (D) from 1 x 4 pine, each measuring 18 inches long.

8. Center the eight slats (D) over the base assembly, spacing them ¼ inch apart. The slats (D) should overhang each of the short horizontals (C) by ⅞ inch, and overhang each of the long horizontals (A) by 1 inch, as shown in figure 2. Apply glue to the meeting surfaces, and nail through each of the eight slats (D) into the horizontals (A and C) and legs (B).

Finishing

9. Fill any cracks, crevices, or nail and screw holes with wood filler, and thoroughly sand all surfaces of the completed footstool.

10. Seal and paint or stain your completed footstool the color of your choice. Here, we painted the footstool to match the Adirondack Chair, seen on page 31.

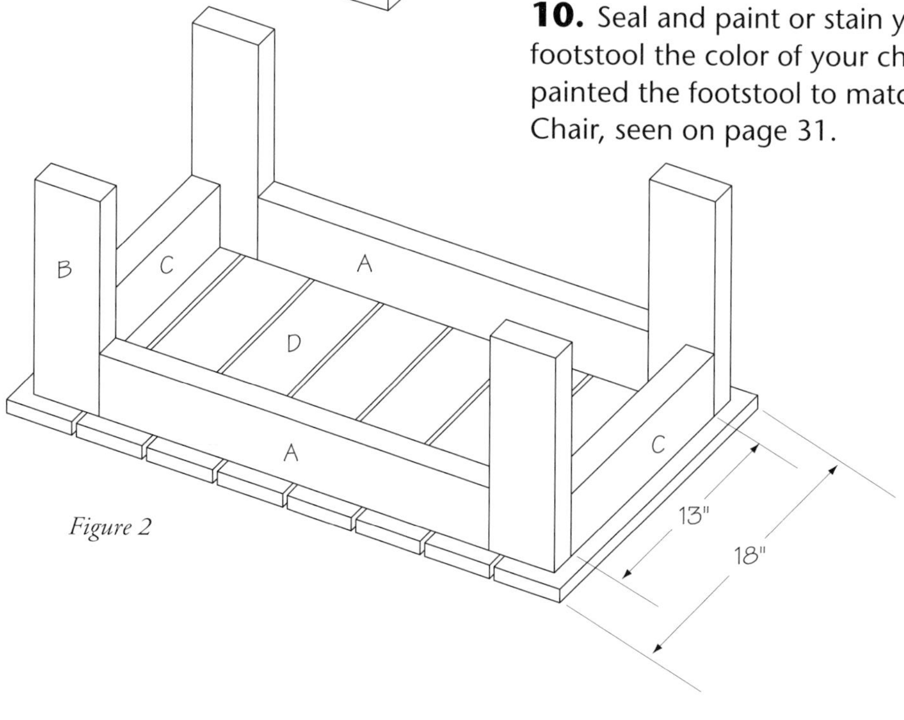

Figure 2

PLANT PEDESTAL

We had fun designing a simple and easy-to-build pedestal that was attractive and substantial enough to support a healthy fern. Then we finished it to look like marble. The pedestal looks great on a porch or in a corner of a deck.

Materials and Supplies

17 linear feet of 1 x 6 pine

2 linear feet of 1 x 8 pine

2 linear feet of 1 x 10 pine

Marbleizing paint kit (comes in several different colors, and includes instructions)

Hardware

50   3d x 1¼" nails

15   6d x 2" nails

Cutting List

Code	Description	Qty.	Materials	Dimensions
A	Side	4	1 x 6 pine	48" long
B	Small Base	2	1 x 8 pine	7¼" long
C	Large Base	2	1 x 10 pine	9¼" long

Cutting the Pieces

1. Cut four sides (A) from 1 x 6 pine, each 48 inches long. It's essential that you cut the ends perfectly square to avoid creating a tower that leans like the famous one we all know about.

2. Cut two small base pieces (B) from 1 x 8 pine, each 7¼ inches long.

3. Cut two large base pieces (C) from 1 x 10 pine, each 9¼ inches long.

Assembly

4. Assemble the four side pieces (A), overlapping each piece in rotation, as shown in figure 1. With the four sides (A) in position, the stand measures 6¼ inches wide on all sides. Nail all four sides (A) along their entire length, using the 3d nails, spaced about 6 inches apart. Countersink the nails.

5. Center one small base (B) over one large base (C), as shown in figure 2. Nail the two pieces together using 3d nails. Countersink the nails.

6. Repeat step 5 using the other small base (B) and large base (C).

7. Center one base assembly on top of the stand. The large base should be facing up (see figure 3). Attach the base to the stand using the larger nails. Countersink the nails.

8. Turn the stand over and repeat step 7 to attach the remaining base assembly.

Finishing

9. Fill any cracks, crevices, or nail holes with wood filler, and thoroughly sand all surfaces of the completed pedestal.

10. We finished our plant stand using a purchased marbleizing kit. It was fun to do, and the results are impressive.

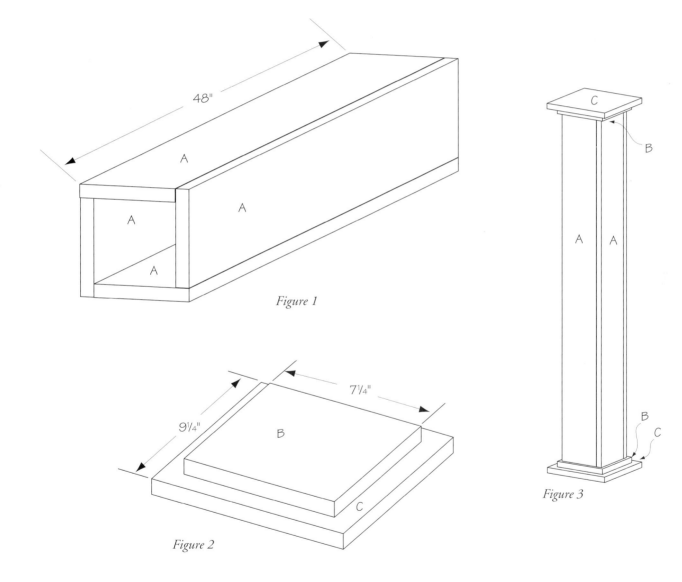

Figure 1

Figure 2

Figure 3

GARDEN CHAIR

Build two of these chairs and group them with our Garden Sofa (page 51), and you'll have a pleasant area for backyard conversation. Or build a single chair, set our Occasional Table (page 84) next to it, and create a great place for drinking iced tea and reading a good book. This comfortable chair is sturdy enough to withstand summer winds, too!

Materials and Supplies

30 linear feet of 2 x 4 pine
8 linear feet of 1 x 4 pine
12 linear feet of 1 x 2 pine

Hardware

50   3d x 1¼" nails
25   2½" screws
30   3½" screws

Cutting List

CODE	DESCRIPTION	QTY.	MATERIALS	DIMENSIONS
A	Horizontal Side	4	2 x 4 pine	15½" long
B	Long Vertical Side	2	2 x 4 pine	35" long
C	Short Vertical Side	2	2 x 4 pine	29" long
D	Outer Seat Support	2	2 x 4 pine	20" long
E	Inner Seat Support	2	2 x 4 pine	19½" long
F	Wide Slat	4	1 x 4 pine	20" long
G	Narrow Slat	2	1 x 2 pine	20" long
H	Horizontal Back	2	2 x 4 pine	20" long
I	Back Slat	7	1 x 2 pine	10" long

Constructing the Chair Sides

1. Cut four horizontal sides (A) from 2 x 4 pine, each measuring 15½ inches long.

2. Cut two long vertical sides (B) from 2 x 4 pine, each measuring 35 inches long.

3. Cut two short vertical sides (C) from 2 x 4 pine, each measuring 29 inches long.

4. Place two horizontal sides (A) parallel to each other, and between one long vertical side (B) and one short vertical side (C), as shown in

figure 1. The top horizontal side (A) is exactly even with the end of the short vertical side (C), and the bottom horizontal side is 14 inches from the other end of that same vertical side (C), as shown in figure 1. Apply glue to the meeting surfaces, and screw at an angle through the edges of the horizontal sides (A) into both the long and short vertical sides (B and C), using two 3½-inch-long screws on each joint.

5. Repeat step 4 to assemble the other side.

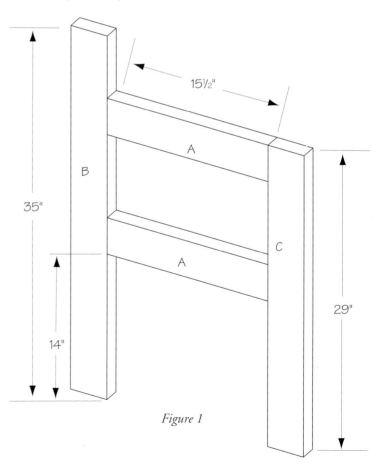

Figure 1

Adding the Seat

6. Cut two outer seat supports (D) from 2 x 4 pine, each measuring 20 inches long.

7. For the next step you may want to ask a willing helper to assist. If no one is available, use a bar clamp to hold the assembly while you screw it together. Place the side assemblies on one 35-inch-long edge, parallel to each other and 20 inches apart. Fit one outer seat support (D) between the two side assemblies, 14 inches from the upper edge of the two side assemblies. The top edge of the outer seat support (D) should be exactly even with the top edge of the lower horizontal side (A), as shown in figure 2. Screw through the side assemblies into the ends of the outer seat supports (D), using two 2½-inch-long screws on each joint.

8. Turn the assembly upside down and attach the remaining outer seat support (D) to the opposite side of the side assemblies, in the same manner that you used in step 7.

9. Cut two inner seat supports (E) from 2 x 4 pine, each measuring 19½ inches long.

10. Fit one inner seat support (E)—wide surface up—between the two outer seat supports (D), ½ inch below the top edge of the lower horizontal side (A), as shown in figure 3. Screw through both of the outer seat supports (D) into the ends of the inner seat support (E), using two 2½-inch-long screws. Also screw through the lower horizontal side (A) into the edge of the inner seat support (E), using three 2½-inch-long screws spaced evenly along the joint.

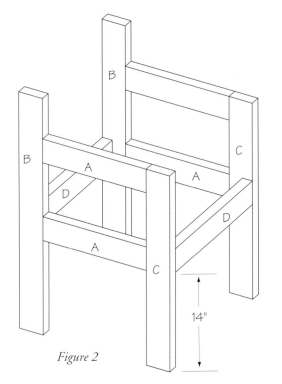

Figure 2

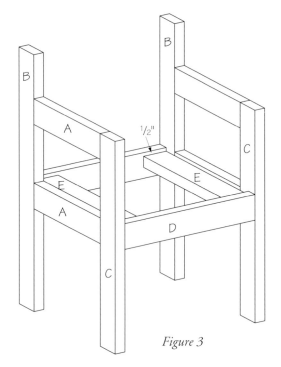

Figure 3

11. Repeat step 10 to attach the remaining inner seat support (E) on the opposite side of the chair.

Adding the Seat Slats

12. The chair seat is comprised of two different widths of wood that are alternated. Cut four wide slats (F) from 1 x 4 pine, each measuring 20 inches long.

13. Cut two narrow slats (G) from 1 x 2 pine, each measuring 20 inches long.

14. Begin by placing a wide slat (F) over the seat support (E) on the front of the chair. Then place a narrow slat (G) next to it. Continue alternating the wide and narrow slats, ending with two wide slats (F) at the back of the chair, as shown in figure 6 on page 46. Adjust the spacing so that the slats are approximately ⅜ inch apart. Nail through each of the slats (F and G) into the seat supports (E). Use two 1¼-inch-long nails on each end of the wide slats (F), and one 1¼-inch-long nail on each end of the narrow slats (G).

Constructing the Chair Back

15. Cut two horizontal backs (H) from 2 x 4 pine, each measuring 20 inches long.

16. Cut a ¾-inch-wide dado, ½ inch deep down the length of one 20-inch-long edge of each of the horizontal backs (H), as shown in figure 4.

17. Cut seven back slats (I) from 1 x 2 pine, each measuring 10 inches long.

18. Working on a level surface, place the horizontal backs (H) parallel to each other, with the dadoes to the inside, as shown in figure 5. Fit the ends of the seven back slats (I) into the dadoes in each of the two horizontal backs (H). The spacing between the slats should be a little over 1½ inches; try using an extra slat as a spacer. When the back slats (I) are properly fitted into the dadoes, the distance between the two horizontal backs (H) should measure 9 inches. The two outer back slats (I) should be even with the ends of the horizontal backs. When the position is perfect, the overall measurements of the back assembly should be 16 inches high and 20 inches wide. Apply glue to the meeting surfaces, and secure the slats by nailing through the dadoed edge of the horizontal backs (H) into the ends of the back slats (I), using two 1¼-inch-long nails on each joint.

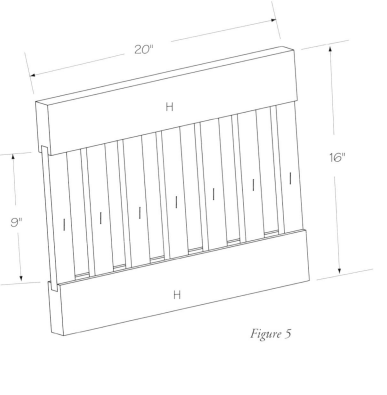

Figure 5

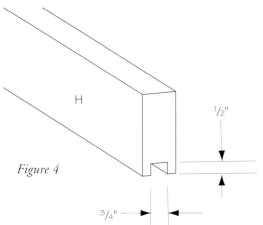

Figure 4

19. Now you are ready to fit the back assembly between the two sides. To make the chair more comfortable, the back assembly is tilted at an angle—out at the top and in at the bottom. The tilt angle is determined by the width of the 2 x 4 on the side assemblies. The lower edge of the back is fitted flush with the front edge of the long vertical sides (B), and the upper edge of the back is fitted flush with the back edge of the long vertical sides (B), as shown in figure 6. When you have the back fitted perfectly, secure the assembly with bar clamps. Screw through the long vertical sides (B) into the ends of the horizontal backs (H), using two 3½-inch-long screws on each joint.

Finishing

20. Fill any cracks, crevices, or screw holes with wood filler, and thoroughly sand all surfaces of the completed chair.

21. Seal and paint or stain your chair the color of your choice.

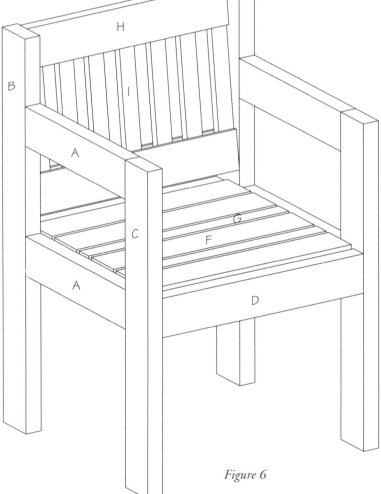

Figure 6

PLANTER TRIO

These attractive and handy planters are at home either inside or out. We finished ours to place on a covered porch, but they would look terrific on a deck or indoors in front of a picture window. We made two small planters and one large one, but you can make any combination you wish and either attach them to one another or use them individually.

Materials and Supplies

For the large planter box:

6 linear feet of 1 x 8 pine

18 linear feet of 1 x 2 pine

12 linear feet of 2 x 2 pine

For the small planter box:

(Remember to double this amount if you intend to make two.)

4 linear feet of 1 x 8 pine

10 linear feet of 1 x 2 pine

10 linear feet of 2 x 2 pine

Hardware (for each planter box)

25 4d x 1½" nails

20 1⅝" screws

Cutting List

For the large planter box:

Code	Description	Qty.	Materials	Dimensions
A	Side	2	1 x 8 pine	7¼" long
B	Front/Back	2	1 x 8 pine	22" long
C	Long Leg	4	2 x 2 pine	32½" long
D	Shelf Side	2	1 x 2 pine	7¼" long
E	Shelf Front/Back	2	1 x 2 pine	22" long
F	Slat	18	1 x 2 pine	7¼" long

For the small planter box:

Code	Description	Qty.	Materials	Dimensions
A	Side	2	1 x 8 pine	7¼" long
G	Small Front/Back	2	1 x 8 pine	12" long
H	Short Leg	4	2 x 2 pine	27½" long
D	Shelf Side	2	1 x 2 pine	7¼" long
I	Small Shelf Front/Back	2	1 x 2 pine	12" long
F	Slat	8	1 x 2 pine	7¼" long

Making the Large Planter Box

1. Cut two sides (A) from 1 x 8 pine, each measuring 7¼ inches long.

2. Cut two long front/backs (B) from 1 x 8 pine, each measuring 22 inches long.

3. Place the two sides (A) on a flat surface, parallel to each other and 20½ inches apart. Place the two front/backs (B) over the ends of the sides (A), as shown in figure 1. Screw through the ends of the front/backs (B) into the ends of the sides (A).

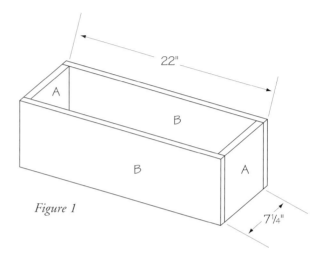

22"

7¼"

Figure 1

Adding the Legs

4. Cut four planter legs (C) from 2 x 2 pine, each measuring 32½ inches long.

5. Fit one planter leg (C) in each corner of the open-ended planter box, 1 inch from what will be the top of the planter (decision time!), as shown in figure 2. Screw through the front/back (B) and side (A) into each leg (C), using 1⅝-inch-long screws. Use two screws on each joint.

Adding the Lower Shelf

6. Cut two shelf sides (D) from 1 x 2 pine, each measuring 7¼ inches long.

7. Attach one shelf side (D) 7½ inches from the bottom of the two legs (C), as shown in figure 3. Screw through the shelf side (D) into each leg (C), using a 1⅝-inch-long screw. Repeat this procedure to attach the other shelf side (D) to the opposite legs (C).

8. Cut two shelf front/backs (E) from 1 x 2 pine, each measuring 22 inches long.

9. Fit one shelf front/back (E) over the ends of the two shelf sides (D), as shown in figure 3. Screw through the shelf front/back (E) into the legs (C), using a 1⅝-inch-long screw. Repeat this procedure to attach the other shelf front/back (E) over the opposite ends of the two shelf sides (D).

Adding the Slats

10. Cut 18 slats (F) from 1 x 2 pine, each measuring 7¼ inches long. Nine slats will be used to make the bottom of the planter box, and nine will be used to make the lower shelf.

11. To fashion the lower shelf, attach the first slat (F) between the shelf front/backs (E), flush with the inside of the legs (C) and with one face even with the top edge of the shelf front/backs (E). Nail through the shelf front/backs (E) into the end of the slat (F), using two 1½-inch-long nails on each joint.

12. Attach the second slat (F) to the opposite side of the shelf.

13. Attach seven more slats (F) between the shelf front/backs (E), spacing them ½ inch apart.

14. Attach the remaining nine slats (F) between the front/back (A) at the bottom of the planter box. The lower surface of the slats (F) should be flush with the bottom of the planter box, as shown in figure 4 on page 50.

Making the Small Planter Box

15. Cut two sides (A) from 1 x 8 pine, each measuring 7¼ inches long.

16. Cut two small front/backs (G) from 1 x 8 pine, each measuring 12 inches long.

17. Place the two sides (A) on a flat surface, parallel to each other and 10½ inches apart. Place the two small front/backs (G) over the ends of the sides (A). Screw through the ends of the small front/backs (G) into the ends of the sides (A).

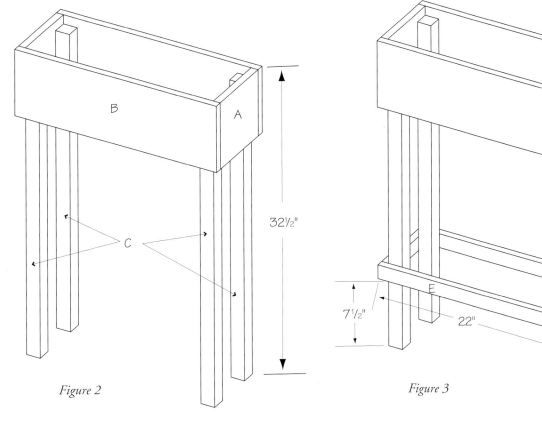

Figure 2

Figure 3

Adding the Legs

18. Cut four short legs (H) from 2 x 2 pine, each measuring 27½ inches long.

19. Fit one short leg (H) in each corner of the open-ended planter box, 1 inch from what will be the top of the planter, as shown in figure 1 on page 48. Screw through the small front/back (G) and side (A) into the short leg (H), using 1⅝-inch-long screws. Use two screws on each joint.

Adding the Lower Shelf

20. Cut two shelf sides (D) from 1 x 2 pine, each measuring 7¼ inches long.

21. Attach one shelf side (D) 7½ inches from the bottom of the two short legs (H), as shown in figure 2 on page 49. Screw through the shelf side (D) into each short leg (H), using a 1⅝-inch-long screw. Repeat to attach the other shelf side (D) to the two opposite short legs (H).

22. Cut two small shelf front/backs (I) from 1 x 2 pine, each measuring 12 inches long.

23. Fit one small shelf front/back (I) over the ends of the shelf sides (D), as shown in figure 3 on page 49. Screw through the small shelf front/back (I) into the short legs (H), using a 1⅝-inch-long screw. Repeat to attach the other shelf front/back (I).

Adding the Slats

24. Cut eight slats (F) from 1 x 2 pine, each measuring 7¼ inches long. Four slats will be used to make the bottom of the planter box, and four will be used to make the lower shelf.

25. To make the lower shelf, attach the first slat (F) between the small shelf front/backs (I), flush with the inside of the short legs (H), as shown in figure 4. Nail through each small shelf front/back (I) into the end of the slat (F), using two 1½-inch-long nails on each joint.

26. Attach the second slat (F) to the opposite side of the shelf.

27. Attach two more slats (F) between the first and second slats (F), spacing them ½ inch apart.

28. Attach the remaining four slats (F) between the small front/back (G) at the bottom of the planter box. The lower surface of the slats (F) should be flush with the bottom of the planter box.

Finishing

29. Fill any cracks, crevices, or screw holes with wood filler, and thoroughly sand all surfaces of the completed planters.

30. Paint or stain the finished project the color of your choice, or simply seal it with a waterproof sealer for a natural look.

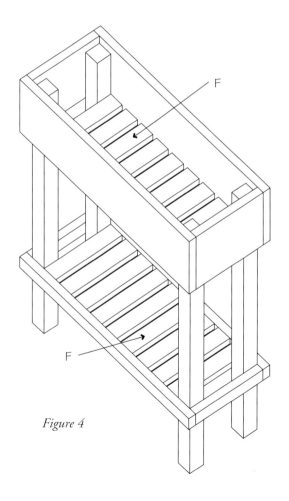

Figure 4

GARDEN SOFA
This sofa would be at home in a garden, on a patio, or on a boat dock. It is constructed of pressure-treated wood so it can withstand the weather. The slats on the seat make the sofa comfortable and assure that rain will not puddle on top of it.

Special Tools and Techniques

Dadoes

Bar Clamps

Materials and Supplies

62 linear feet of 2 x 4 pine

20 linear feet of 1 x 4 pine

30 linear feet of 1 x 2 pine

Hardware

30	3-1/2" screws
30	2-1/2" screws
160	3d x 1¼" nails
60	4d x 1½" nails

Cutting List

Code	Description	Qty.	Materials	Dimensions
A	Horizontal Side	4	2 x 4 pine	15½" long
B	Long Vertical Side	2	2 x 4 pine	35" long
C	Short Vertical Side	2	2 x 4 pine	29" long
D	Outer Seat Support	2	2 x 4 pine	59" long
E	Inner Seat Support	5	2 x 4 pine	19½" long
F	Wide Slat	4	1 x 4 pine	59" long
G	Narrow Slat	2	1 x 2 pine	59" long
H	Horizontal Back	2	2 x 4 pine	59" long
I	Back Slat	20	1 x 2 pine	10" long

Constructing the Sofa Sides

1. Cut four horizontal sides (A) from 2 x 4 pine, each measuring 15½ inches long.

2. Cut two long vertical sides (B) from 2 x 4 pine, each measuring 35 inches long.

3. Cut two short vertical sides (C) from 2 x 4 pine, each measuring 29 inches long.

4. Place two horizontal sides (A) parallel to each other, and between one long vertical side (B) and one short vertical side (C), as shown in figure 1. The top horizontal side (A) is exactly even with the end of the short vertical side (C) and the bottom horizontal side (A), and is 14 inches from the other end of that same vertical side (C), as shown in figure 1. Toenail through the edges of the horizontal sides (A), into both the long and short vertical sides (B and C), using two 3½-inch-long screws on each joint.

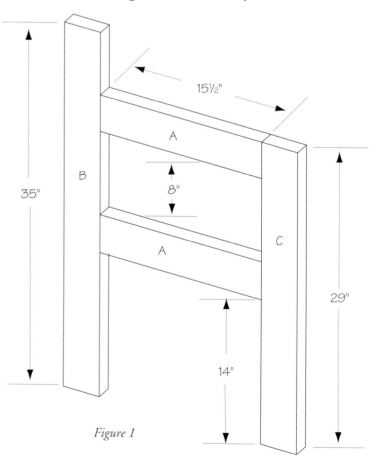

Figure 1

5. Repeat step 4 to assemble the second side.

Adding the Seat

6. Cut two outer seat supports (D) from 2 x 4 pine, each measuring 59 inches long.

7. For the next step, you may want to ask a willing helper to assist. If no one is available (or willing), use a bar clamp to hold the assembly while you screw it together. Place each side assembly on its long vertical edge (B), 59 inches away from the other side, as shown in figure 2. Fit the front outer seat support (D) between the two short vertical sides (C), 14 inches from the upper edge of the sides. The top edge of the front outer seat support (D) should be exactly even with the top edge of the lower horizontal side (A). Screw through the side assemblies into the ends of the outer seat support (D), using two 2½-long screws on each joint.

8. Repeat step 7 to attach the other outer seat support (D) to the back of the sofa between the side assemblies, as shown in figure 2. The top edge of the outer seat support (D) should be exactly even with the top edge of the lower horizontal sides (A). Using two 2½-inch-long screws on each joint, screw through the long vertical sides (B) into the ends of the outer seat supports.

9. Cut five inner seat supports (E) from 2 x 4 pine, measuring 19½ inches long.

10. Turn the assembly right side up. As shown in figure 3, position one inner seat support (E) wide side up, between the two outer seat supports (D) and against one horizontal side (A), ¾ inch below the top of the outer seat supports (D). Screw through the outer seat supports (D) into the end of the inner seat support (E), using two 2½-inch-long screws.

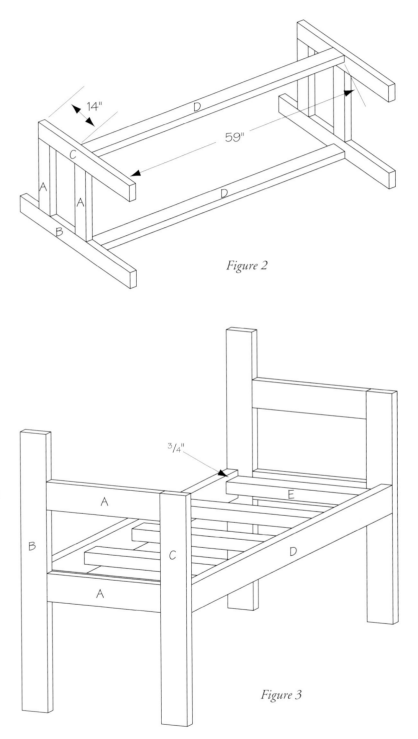

Figure 2

Figure 3

11. Repeat this step with another inner seat support (E), placed at the other end of the outer seat supports.

12. Fit the remaining three inner seat supports (E) between the outer seat supports (D). Center one inner seat support (E), and space the other two evenly, as shown in figure 3 on page 53. Remember to place them ¾ inch below the top of the outer seat supports (D). Screw through the outer seat supports (D) into the ends of the inner seat supports (E), using two 2½-inch-long screws on each joint.

Adding the Seat Slats

13. The sofa seat is comprised of two different widths of wood that are alternated. Cut four wide slats (F) from 1 x 4 pine, each measuring 59 inches long.

14. Cut two narrow slats (G) from 1 x 2 pine, each measuring 59 inches long.

15. Begin by placing a wide slat (F) over the seat supports (E) on the front of the sofa. Then place a narrow slat (G) next to it. Continue alternating the wide and narrow slats, ending with two wide slats (F) at the back of the sofa, as shown in figure 6 on page 55. Adjust the spac-

ing so that the slats are approximately ⅜ inch apart. Nail through each of the slats (F and G) into the seat supports (E), securing each of the slats to one of the seat supports (E). Use two 1½-inch-long nails on each joint.

Constructing the Sofa Back

16. Cut two horizontal backs (H) from 2 x 4 pine, each measuring 59 inches long.

17. Cut a ¾-inch-wide dado, ½ inch deep, down the length of one 59-inch edge of each of the horizontal backs (H), as shown in figure 4.

18. Cut 20 back slats (I) from 1 x 2 pine, each measuring 10 inches long.

19. Working on a level surface, place the horizontal backs (H) parallel to each other, with the dadoes to the inside, as shown in figure 5. Fit the ends of the 20 back slats (I) into the dadoes in each of the two horizontal backs (H). The spacing between the slats should be approximately 1½ inches. In fact, we used an extra slat as a spacer. When the back slats (I) are properly fitted into the dadoes, the distance between the two horizontal backs (H) should be 9 inches. The two outer back slats (I) should be even with the ends of the horizontal backs (H). When the posi-

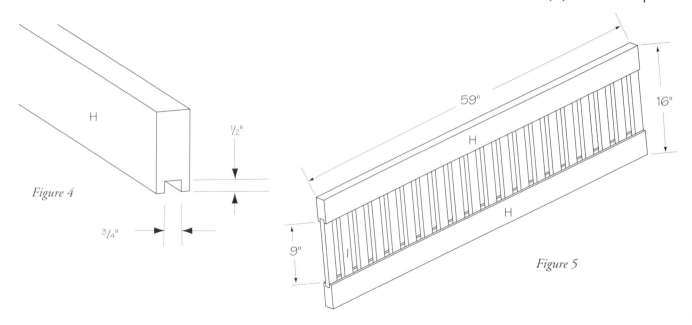

Figure 4

Figure 5

tion is perfect, the overall measurements of the back assembly should be 16 inches high and 59 inches wide. Secure the slats by nailing through the dadoed edge of the horizontal back (H) into the ends of the back slats (I), using two 1¼-inch-long nails on each joint.

20. Turn the assembly over and repeat the nailing procedure on the other side.

21. It is now time to fit the back assembly between the two sides. To make the sofa more comfortable, the back assembly is tilted at an angle—out at the top and in at the bottom. The tilt angle is determined by the width of the 2 x 4 on the side assemblies. The lower edge of the back is fitted flush with the inside edge of the

long vertical sides (B); the upper edge of the back is fitted flush with the outer edge of the long vertical sides (B), as shown in figure 6. When you have the back fitted perfectly, secure the assembly with bar clamps. Screw through the long vertical sides (B) into the ends of the horizontal backs (H), using two 3½-inch-long screws on each joint.

Finishing the Sofa

22. Fill any cracks, crevices, or screw holes with wood filler, and thoroughly sand all surfaces of the completed sofa.

23. Seal and paint or stain your sofa the color of your choice.

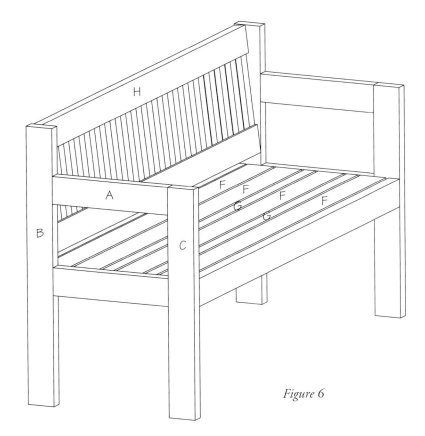

Figure 6

CUPOLA BIRDHOUSE

This whimsical birdhouse is mounted on our deck. It's such a treat watching the birds carry twigs into their house to build the nest! Even if you're not a bird watcher, you'll enjoy seeing this birdhouse in your garden or on your patio.

Materials and Supplies

1 piece of ½"-thick exterior plywood, measuring 12" x 24"

1 piece of ⅜"-thick exterior plywood, measuring 12" x 36"

3 linear feet of 1 x 8 pine

15 linear feet of 1 x 4 pine

1 linear foot of 1 x 2 pine

1 decorative curtain rod finial

3 linear feet of 2"-wide canvas fabric strips

Staple gun and staples

Paneling adhesive

Hardware

20   4d x 1½" nails

20   1¼" screws

Cutting List

Code	Description	Qty.	Materials	Dimensions
A	Top/Bottom	2	½" plywood	11¼" diameter circle
B	Wide Side	10	1 x 4 pine	11" long
C	Narrow Side	1	1 x 2 pine	11" long
D	Base Side	4	1 x 4 pine	14½" long
E	Base	2	1 x 8 pine	16" long
F	Roof Panel	8	⅜" plywood	12" x 12" x 7" triangle

Making the House

1. Cut two top/bottoms (A) from ½-inch-thick plywood, each a circle measuring 11¼ inches in diameter.

2. Cut 10 wide sides (B) from 1 x 4 pine, each measuring 11 inches long.

3. Cut a 1½-inch-diameter hole in one wide side (B), 4 inches from one end, and centered on the width, as shown in figure 1. (Note: Different birds require different size openings. Refer to a book on building birdhouses to help you determine what size hole to drill. The hole size used here is a good match for flycatchers, wrens, nuthatches, and tree swallows.)

4. Measure carefully and mark the center of the 1 x 4 width of each of the wide sides (B), ⅜ inch from each end, as shown in figure 1.

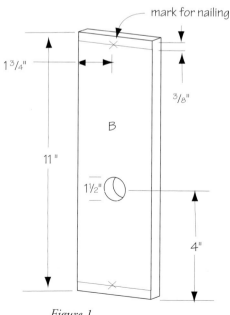

Figure 1

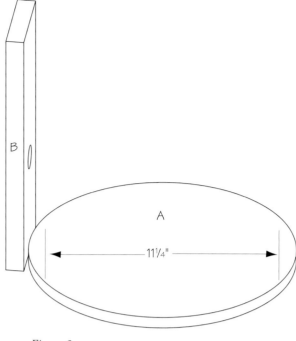

Figure 2

Making the Base

10. Cut four base sides (D) from 1 x 4 pine, each measuring 14½ inches long.

11. Place two bases (D) on a level surface, parallel to each other and 14½ inches apart. Fit the remaining two base sides (D) between the first two base sides (D), as shown in figure 3. Nail through the overlapping base sides (D) into the ends of the inner base sides (D), using two 1½-inch-long nails on each of the joints.

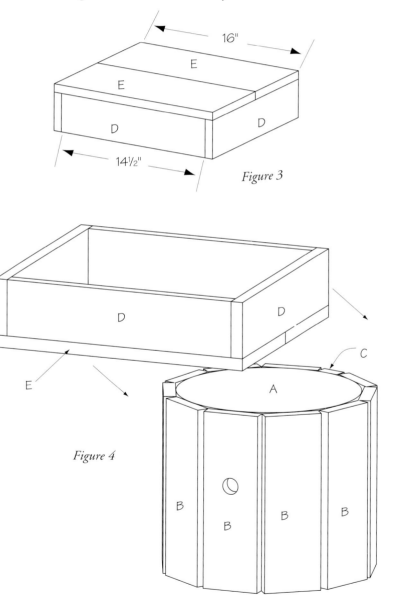

Figure 3

5. Place one top/bottom (A) on a level surface. Attach one wide side (B) to the top/bottom (A). Nail through the mark on the wide side (B) into the edge of the top/bottom (A) using a 1½-inch-long nail, as shown in figure 2.

6. Place a second wide side (B) next to the first one, so that the inner edges meet. Nail through the wide side (B) into the edge of the top/bottom (A). Continue this procedure to attach the remaining eight wide sides (B) to the top/bottom (A).

7. Cut one narrow side (C) from 1 x 2 pine, measuring 11 inches long. Mark the exact center of the width, ⅜ inch from each end.

8. Attach the narrow side (C) to the top/bottom (A) in the space remaining between the first and last wide sides (B). Nail through the mark in the narrow side (C) into the top/bottom (A).

9. Place the remaining top/bottom (A) on a level surface. Turn the house assembly upside down, and fit the narrow and wide sides (B and C) over the remaining top/bottom (A). Nail through the marks to attach each of the sides (B and C) to the top/bottom (A).

Figure 4

12. Cut two bases (E) from 1 x 8 pine, each measuring 16 inches long.

13. Fit the two bases (E) over the base sides (D), as shown in figure 3. Apply glue to the meeting surfaces, and nail through the edges of the two bases (E) into the base sides (D). Use four or five 1½-inch-long nails on each side.

14. Place the house assembly on a level surface, with the drilled hole closer to the top.

15. Turn the base assembly upside down and center it over the house assembly, as shown in figure 4. Apply glue to the meeting surfaces, and screw through both bases (E) into the top/bottom (A), using five or six 1¼-inch screws.

Making the Roof

16. Cut eight triangular roof panels (F) from ⅜-inch thick plywood, each panel measuring 12 x 12 x 7 inches. These will be joined together to form an eight-sided cone for the roof.

17. To hold the pieces together temporarily, we used small strips of canvas fabric and a staple gun.

18. Begin by placing two roof panels (F) on a flat surface, with their 12 inch sides exactly matching, as shown in figure 5. Cut two 2-inch-long strips of canvas fabric. Place one strip about 2 inches from the top, and one strip about 1 inch from the bottom of the panels. Use a staple gun to staple the fabric to each of the two roof panels (F). Repeat until you have attached the remaining six roof panels (F) to the first two.

19. Now comes the awkward part. You may wish to enlist the assistance of a friend for this step. Have someone hold the assembly so that you can connect the first roof panel to the eighth roof panel. Again use two fabric strips to connect the panels.

20. Place the connected roof right side up on a level surface. Adjust the panels so that the assembly is even on all sides. Then apply paneling adhesive into each of the joints to form a smooth surface. Let the assembly dry overnight.

Finishing

21. As a finishing touch, we glued a curtain rod finial to the top of the roof.

22. If you plan to have visitors to your new birdhouse, it's best to attach the roof to the house assembly with a hinge so that you can clean it out after one family of birds has come and gone. If you plan to use the birdhouse as an outdoor ornament, simply nail through the roof into the house assembly.

23. Fill any cracks, crevices, or screw holes with wood filler, and thoroughly sand all surfaces of the completed birdhouse.

24. Seal and paint or stain your birdhouse the colors of your choice.

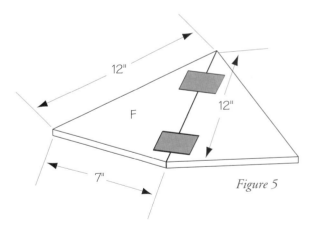

12"

12"

F

7"

Figure 5

COTTAGE MAILBOX

When we bought our house it came complete with a standard boring mailbox. When we shopped for a new one we discovered that all the good-looking mailboxes had a very healthy price tag attached to them. So we covered our standard boring mailbox with inexpensive plywood and, we think, a few delightful details. We're very happy with the result, and the mailbox brings smiles to people passing by.

Special Tools and Techniques

Beveling

Materials and Supplies

½ sheet of ⅜"-thick exterior plywood, measuring 4' x 4'

2 linear feet of 2 x 4 pine

11 picket fence sections*

6-10 plants in 3" pots (optional)

Premade numbers for your address

Standard size mailbox

*Premade pickets are available at most hobby and craft-supply stores, or you can construct your own (see Adding the Fencing on page 63).

Hardware

60   3d x 1" nails

10   1½" screws

Cutting List

Code	Description	Qty.	Materials	Dimensions
A	Front	1	⅜" plywood	11¼" x 13"
B	Back	1	⅜" plywood	11¼" x 13"
C	Sides	2	⅜" plywood	18¾" x 9¾"
D	Roof	2	⅜" plywood	9¼" x 23½"
E	Chimney	1	2 x 4 pine	14" long
F	Base	2	⅜" plywood	9¾" x 6½"

Making the Front, Back, and Sides

1. Cut one front (A) from ⅜-inch-thick plywood, measuring 11¼ x 13 inches.

2. Refer to figure 1 to cut a curved doorway and a peaked roof on the front (A). Double-check to make certain that the curved doorway is sized to accommodate your mailbox.

3. Cut one back (B) from ⅜-inch-thick plywood, measuring 11¼ x 13 inches.

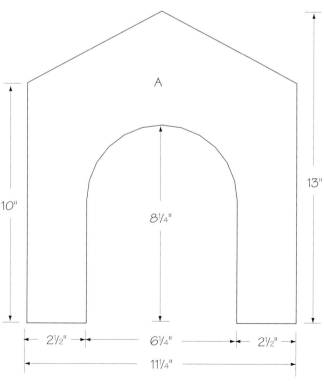

Figure 1

4. Use the front (A) as a pattern to cut a peaked roof on the back (B). Do not cut the curved doorway on the back (B).

5. Cut two sides (C) from ⅜-inch-thick plywood, each measuring 18¾ x 9¾ inches.

6. Place the two sides (C) on a level surface, parallel to each other and 11¼ inches apart. The 18¾-inch-long edge of the sides should face down. Fit the front (A) and back (B) between the two sides (D), as shown in figure 2. Note that the sides (C) will be slightly shorter at the top edges than the front (A) and back (B). That distance will allow for the angle of the roof peak. Apply glue to the meeting surfaces and use four 1-inch-long nails on each joint.

Adding the Roof

7. Cut two roofs (D) from ⅜-inch-thick plywood, each measuring 9¼ x 23¼ inches.

8. Bevel one 23¼-inch edge of each of the roofs (D) at a 30-degree angle, as shown in figure 3 on page 63.

9. Fit the two roofs (D) over the sides (C), front (A), and back (B), matching the bevels. The roofs (D) should overhang the front (A) and back (B) an equal amount. Nail through the roof (D) into the front, back, and sides (A, B, and C), using 1-inch-long nails.

Adding the Chimney

10. Cut one chimney (E) from 2 x 4 pine, measuring 14 inches long.

11. Measure 9¾ inches from one end of the chimney (E), mark the spot, and cut across the width of the chimney (E) at a 30-degree angle, as shown in figure 4 on page 63.

12. Fit the shorter portion of the chimney (E) on top of the roof (D), just above where the longer portion of the chimney will fit. Screw through the underside of the roof (D) into the short chimney, using two 1½-inch-long screws. Countersink the screws.

13. Fit the longer portion of the chimney (E) under the roof against one side of the house.

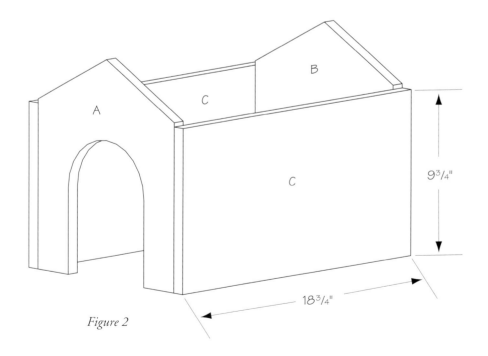

Figure 2

Screw through the inside of the side (C) into the chimney (E), using two 1½-inch long screws. (Note: The longer portion of the chimney is not visible in the project photograph.)

Adding the Base

14. Cut two bases (F) from ⅜-inch-thick plywood, each measuring 19¾ x 6½ inches.

15. Attach one base (F) to the right bottom of the house assembly, flush with the inside with the front door and extending 1 inch from the house front. Apply glue to the meeting surfaces and nail through the base (F) into the edges of the front, back, and side (A, B, and C), using 1-inch-long nails spaced every three inches.

16. Repeat step 15 to attach the remaining base (F) to the left side of the house.

Adding the Fencing

17. We purchased premade sections of white picket fence at a hobby store. Each section is 6½ inches long.

If you prefer to make your own picket fence, simply cut two ⅝-inch-wide strips, each measuring 6½ inches long. These will be the fence rails.

Then cut eight pickets from ⅝-inch-wide strips, each measuring 4 inches long. Space the pickets evenly over the two fence rails and glue and nail together using small brads.

18. Cut and fit the picket fence sections to fit all the way around both of the bases.

Finishing

19. Remove the flag from the old mailbox and attach it to the top of the chimney.

20. Fill any cracks, crevices, or screw holes with wood filler, and thoroughly sand all surfaces of the completed mailbox.

21. Seal and paint or stain your mailbox the colors of your choice.

22. Attach the numbers for your address on the side of the mailbox.

23. Slip the cottage mailbox over your purchased mailbox.

24. As a final decorative touch, we placed several live plants in 3-inch containers in our mailbox "yard."

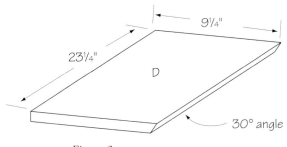

Figure 3

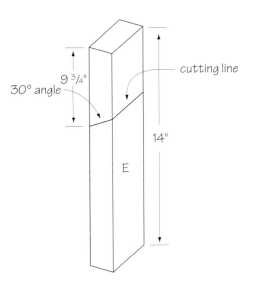

Figure 4

DINING TABLE

We love outdoor cooking and dining with friends and family, but we ran out of room at our poolside table. So we built a new one! Now we have ample space to accommodate the food off the grill—and lots of neighbors, too! The tile top allows you to coordinate the table color with the rest of your outdoor furnishings.

Special Tools and Techniques

Dadoes

Miters

Metal trowel

Rubber-surface trowel

Tile cutter

Materials and Supplies

10 linear feet of 4 x 4 pine

24 linear feet of 2 x 4 pine

14 linear feet of 1 x 2 pine

20 linear feet of 1 x 8 pine

1 piece of ⅜"-thick exterior plywood, measuring 52" x 28"

4 wooden finials*

Tile to cover an area 66½" x 39½"*

Tile grout

Tile mastic

Tile sealer

Hardware

125   2½" screws

50   1¼" screws

*Notes on Materials

The wooden finials we used for the table "feet" are designed to be used on a fence post. They can be purchased at most building-supply stores, and have a large screw already attached in the center. The ones we used are 3 inches tall. You can substitute any exterior-rated finial you like, but if it's taller than 3 inches, be sure to adjust the length of your legs accordingly, or your completed table will not be the correct height.

When choosing tile for this table, consider that you must cover an area measuring 52" x 28." If the tile you purchased doesn't fit within these dimensions, you can either alter the dimensions of the table or—use our much easier solution—simply cut the tiles into interesting shapes.

To install the tile, you need a plain, metal trowel for spreading the mastic and a rubber-surfaced trowel for applying the grout. If you need to trim the tile to fit the table, or want to cut them into pieces for a mosaic effect as we did with our table, you will also need a tile cutter.

Cutting List

CODE	DESCRIPTION	QTY.	MATERIALS	DIMENSIONS
A	Leg	4	4 x 4 pine	26" long
B	Long Side	2	2 x 4 pine	55" long
C	Short Sides	2	2 x 4 pine	31" long
D	Center Support	3	2 x 4 pine	8" long
E	Short Inner Support	8	1 x 2 pine	11⅞" long
F	Long Inner Support	2	1 x 2 pine	26½" long
G	Long Trim	2	1 x 8 pine	66½" long
H	Short Trim	2	1 x 8 pine	42½" long
I	Top	1	⅜" plywood	52" x 28"

Making the Legs

1. Cut four legs (A) from 4 x 4 pine, each measuring 26 inches long.

2. In order to properly support the table, the legs must be dadoed. Refer to figure 1 to dado the end of one leg (A). Note that the dado is 1½ inches deep on each side, and 3½ inches long.

3. Repeat step 2 to dado the ends of the remaining three legs (A).

Adding the Table Sides

4. Cut two long sides (B) from 2 x 4 pine, each measuring 55 inches long.

5. Miter each end of the long sides (B) at a 45-degree angle, as shown in figure 2. Note that the miters are mirror images of each other.

6. Cut two short sides (C) from 2 x 4 pine, each measuring 31 inches long.

7. Miter each end of the short sides (C) at a 45-degree angle, as you did for the long sides (B).

8. Place the long sides (B) parallel to each other on a level surface, with the miters facing in. Fit the short sides (C) between the long sides (B), matching miters on all four corners, as shown in figure 3. Apply glue to the meeting surfaces of the miters, and screw through each mitered joint, using a 2½-inch long screw on each side.

Attaching the Legs

9. Turn one leg (A) dado-side down, and fit the dado over one corner of the side assembly, as shown in figure 4 on page 67. Apply glue on the meeting surfaces, and screw through both the long side (B) and short side (C) into the leg (A). Use two 2½-inch-long screws on each joint.

10. Repeat step 9 three more times to attach the remaining three legs (A) to the three corners of the side assembly.

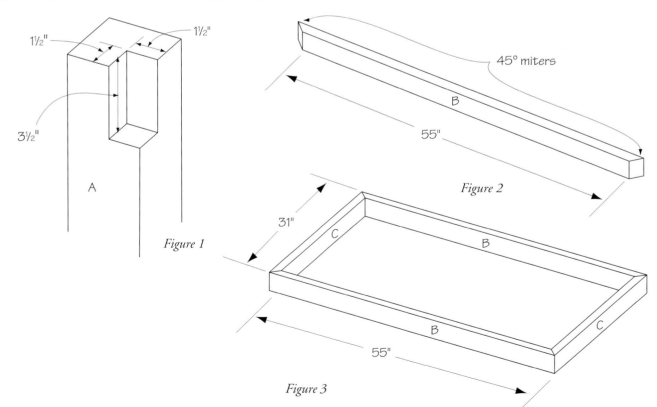

1½" 1½"

3½"

A

Figure 1

45° miters

B

55"

Figure 2

31"

C

B

B

C

55"

Figure 3

11. On the bottom of each leg, we attached a finial designed to top a fence post. Mark the center bottom of each of the legs (A), and screw in a finial.

Adding the Inner Supports

12. Cut three center supports (D) from 2 x 4 pine, each measuring 28 inches long.

13. Fit the three center supports (D) between the two long sides (B), edge up, 11⅞ inches apart, as shown in figure 5. Screw through the long sides (B) into the ends of the inner supports (D). Use two 2½-inch-long screws on each joint.

14. Cut eight short inner supports (E) from 1 x 2 pine, each measuring 11⅞ inches long.

15. Fit one short inner support (E) flush with the top of the long side (B), between the short side (C) and the center support (D), as shown in figure 6. Screw through the short inner support (E) into the long side (B), using three 1¼-inch-long screws. Repeat this process to attach the remaining seven short inner supports (E) to the long sides (B).

16. Cut two long inner supports (F) from 1 x 2 pine, each measuring 26½ inches long.

17. Fit one long inner support (F) flush with the top of each short side (C), as shown in figure 6. Use four or five 1¼-inch-long screws to attach each of these supports (F) to the short sides (C).

Adding the Trim

18. Cut two long trim pieces (G) from 1 x 8 pine, each measuring 66½ inches long.

19. Miter both ends of each of the long trim pieces at opposing 45-degree angles, as shown in figure 7 on page 68.

20. Cut two short trim pieces (H) from 1 x 8 pine, each measuring 42½ inches long.

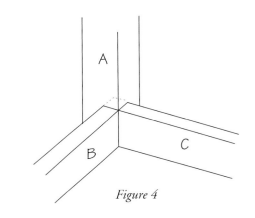

Figure 4

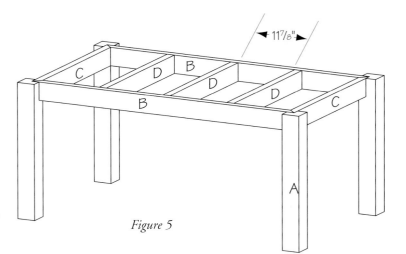

Figure 5

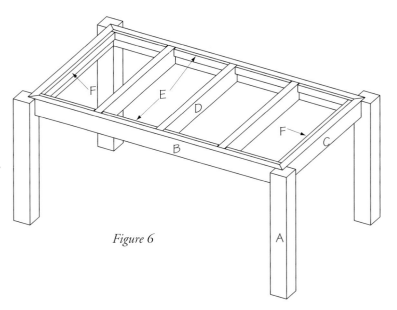

Figure 6

21. Miter both ends of each of the short trim pieces (H) at opposing 45-degree angles, as shown in figure 7.

22. Fit the long trim pieces (G) over the long sides (B), exactly matching the miters, as shown in figure 7. Apply glue to the tops of the long sides (B) and screw through the long trim pieces (G) into the long sides (B), using 1¼-inch-long screws about every four inches.

23. Fit the short trim pieces (H) over the short sides (C), exactly matching the miters. Apply glue to the tops of the short sides (C) and to the miters. Screw through the short trim pieces (H) into the short sides (C), using 1¼-inch-long screws about every four inches. Finally, screw at an angle through the ends of the short trim pieces (G), using one 2½-inch-long screw on each joint.

Adding the Plywood Top

24. Cut one top (I) from ⅜-inch-thick plywood, measuring 52 x 28 inches.

25. Fit the top (I) in the center of the table over the supports. The top sits ⅜ inch lower than the trim pieces (G and H) to allow enough depth for the tile and mastic. Screw through the top (I) into all of the supports (D, E, and F), using 1¼-inch-long screws spaced about every 5 inches.

Adding the Tile

26. Following the manufacturer's directions, carefully spread an even coat of the tile mastic over the surface of the top (I) with a trowel.

27. Place the tiles on the mastic one at a time, making sure that they are positioned correctly. Don't slide the tiles, or the mastic will be forced up on the sides of the tile. Let the mastic dry overnight.

28. Mix the tile grout according to the manufacturer's directions (or use premixed grout).

29. Spread the grout over the tile using a rubber-surfaced trowel held at an angle so that the grout is forced evenly into the spaces between the tiles.

30. Use a damp rag to wipe the excess grout off the tiles and joints; if you let it dry, the hardened grout will be very difficult to remove. Try to use as little water as possible when removing the excess so that you don't thin the grout that remains. Let the grout dry overnight.

31. Rinse the remaining film from the tile and wipe it with an old towel.

32. Apply grout sealer, following the manufacturer's directions.

Finishing

33. Fill all cracks, crevices, and screw holes with wood filler. Thoroughly sand all surfaces of the completed table.

34. We stained our table reddish brown to match our tile grout. You can stain yours a different color, or simply seal it with a waterproof sealer.

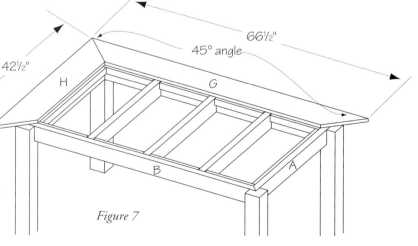

Figure 7

LATTICE BOWER

This romantic bower will become your own personal hideaway. Place it in a quiet corner of the yard, and it's perfect for early morning coffee or late afternoon lounging. The frame is constructed of 2 x 4s, so this beauty is very sturdy.

Special Tools and Techniques

Router

Rabbet bit

Materials and Supplies

140 linear feet of 2 x 4 pine

12 linear feet of 1 x 2 pine

35 linear feet of 1 x 4 pine

3 sheets of lattice, 4' x 8'*

*premade lattice can be purchased at lumber-supply outlets

Hardware

200 2½" screws

25   1½" screws

200 4d x 1½" nails

14   lag bolts, 3" long

Cutting List

Code	Description	Qty.	Materials	Dimensions
A	Vertical	6	2 x 4 pine	72" long
B	Horizontal Side	6	2 x 4 pine	21½" long
C	Slats	19	2 x 4 pine	23½" long
D	Side Panel	2	lattice	23" x 34½"
E	Horizontal Back	3	2 x 4 pine	57" long
F	Back Panel	1	lattice	58½" x 34½"
G	Long Bench Support	2	2 x 4 pine	64" long
H	Short Bench Support	2	2 x 4 pine	24" long
I	Inner Supports	2	1 x 2 pine	61" long
J	Bench Slat	16	1 x 4 pine	24" long
K	Long Top Support	2	2 x 4 pine	64" long
L	Short Top Support	2	2 x 4 pine	24" long
M	Top Panel	1	lattice	62½" x 25½"

Making the Sides

1. Cut two verticals (A) from 2 x 4 pine, each measuring 72 inches long.

2. Cut three horizontal sides (B) from 2 x 4 pine, each measuring 21½ inches long.

3. Place the two verticals (A) on a level surface, wide face up, 21½ inches apart and parallel to each other. Fit the three horizontal sides (B) between the two verticals, spacing them as shown in figure 1. The inside of the top two

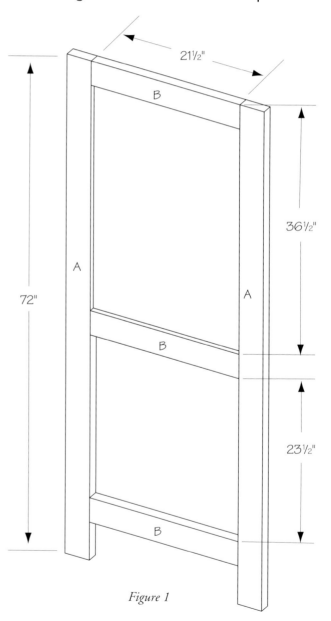

Figure 1

horizontal sides (B) will later be routed ¾ inch deep to accommodate the lattice. Because of this, we need to avoid placing screws where they will interfere with the routing. Mark what will be the inside of the assembly, and avoid placing screws within ¾ inch of that side. Then apply glue to the meeting surfaces, clamp the assembly together securely, and toenail through each side of the horizontal sides (B) into the verticals (A) using two 2½-inch-long screws on each joint.

4. Cut four slats (C) from 2 x 4 pine, each measuring 23½ inches long.

5. Fit the four slats (C) between the two lower horizontal sides (B), as shown in figure 2. Toenail through each side of the slats (C) into each of the two lower horizontal sides (B), using two 2½-inch-long screws on each joint.

6. The upper opening between the two upper horizontal side (B) and the two verticals (A) must be routed to accommodate the lattice panel. Place the assembly with the side you designated as the "inside" face up. Use a rabbet bit to rout the edges ¾ inch deep and ¾ inch wide where the lattice will fit, as shown in figure 2.

7. Before cutting any of your lattice, carefully plan exactly how to position the pieces that you need to cut. Lattice is a little tricky, since it looks like the same design whichever way you look at it. But this is not true. Be sure that you cut it so that the over-and-under lattice panels are the same. Cut the lattice with the grain each time, or, when you place the pieces together, the differences will be obvious. Cut a side panel (D) from lattice, measuring 23 x 34½ inches. Save any lattice slats that are left over from the cutting. These will be used as trim.

8. Apply glue to the meeting surfaces, and fit the side panel (D) into the routed opening on the upper section of the assembled side panel. Use 1½-inch-long finishing nails to attach the lattice to the verticals (A) and horizontal sides (B).

9. Repeat steps 1 through 8 to assemble the other side.

Making the Back

10. Cut two verticals (A) from 2 x 4 pine, each measuring 72 inches long.

11. Cut three horizontal backs (E) from 2 x 4 pine, each measuring 57 inches long.

12. Place the two verticals (A) on a level surface, wide face up, 57 inches apart and parallel

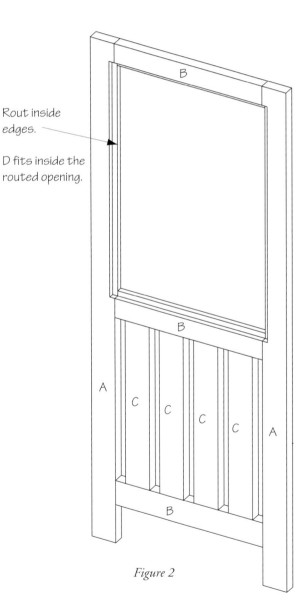

Rout inside edges.

D fits inside the routed opening.

Figure 2

to each other. Fit the three horizontal backs (E) between the two verticals (A), spacing them as shown in figure 1 on page 70. Here, too, the inside edges of the top two horizontal backs (E) will later be routed ¾ inch deep to accommodate the lattice. Because of this, we need to avoid placing screws where they will interfere with the routing. Mark what will be the inside of the assembly, and avoid placing screws within ¾ inch of that side. Then apply glue to the meeting surfaces, clamp the assembly together securely, and toenail through each side of the horizontal backs (E) into the verticals (A), using two 2½-inch-long screws on each joint.

13. Cut 11 slats (C) from 2 x 4 pine, each measuring 23½ inches long.

14. Fit the 11 slats (C) between the two lower horizontal backs (E) in the same manner you used to assemble the sides. Space the slats 1½ inches apart. When you have the spacing correct, toenail through each side of the slats (C) into each of the two lower horizontal backs (E), using two 2½-inch-long screws on each joint.

15. Now the upper opening between the two upper horizontal backs (E) and the two verticals (A) must be routed to accommodate the lattice panel. Place the assembly with the side you designated as the "inside" face up. Use a rabbet bit to rout the edges ¾ inch deep and ¾ inch wide where the lattice will fit.

16. Cut a back panel (F) from lattice, measuring 58½ x 34½ inches. Save the leftover lattice slats for the trim.

17. Fit the back panel (F) into the routed opening on the upper section of the assembled back. Use 1½-inch-long finishing nails to attach the lattice to the verticals (A) and horizontal backs (E).

Connecting the Sides and Back

18. You will probably want to enlist the assistance of a helper for this next maneuver. If one is not available, use bar clamps to hold the pieces in place while you join them. Place the back assembly on a level work surface, with the "inside" surface facing up. Place one side

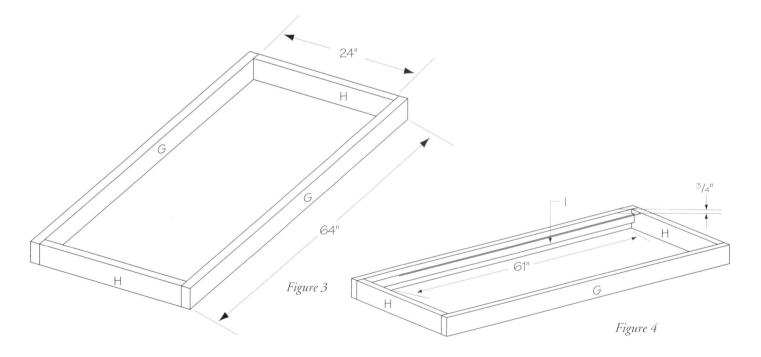

Figure 3

Figure 4

assembly, edge up, next to the back assembly. Predrill and countersink holes, and use three 3-inch-long lag bolts to secure the joint. Place each of the lag bolts opposite each of the horizontal backs (E).

19. Repeat the procedure to attach the other side assembly to the opposite side of the back assembly.

Constructing the Bench

20. Cut two long bench supports (G) from 2 x 4 pine, each measuring 64 inches long.

21. Cut two short bench supports (H) from 2 x 4 pine, each measuring 24 inches long.

22. Place the two long bench supports (G) on a level surface, parallel to each other, and 24 inches apart. Fit the two short bench supports (H) between the two long bench supports (G), as shown in figure 3. Screw through the long bench supports (G) into the ends of the short bench supports (H). Use two 2½-inch-long screws on each of the joints.

23. Cut two inner supports (I) from 1 x 2 pine, each measuring 61 inches long.

24. Apply glue to the meeting surfaces and screw one inner support (I) to the inner side of one long bench support (G), ¾ inch from the top edge, as shown in figure 4. Use 1½-inch-long screws about every 5 inches.

25. Repeat step 24 to attach the other inner support (I) to the opposite long bench support (G).

26. Cut 16 bench slats (J) from 1 x 4 pine, each measuring 24 inches long.

27. Fit the 16 bench slats (J) over the two inner supports (I), leaving approximately ¼ inch between bench slats (J), as shown in figure 5. When you are satisfied with the placement, nail through each bench slat (J) into the inner supports (I), using two 1½-inch-long nails on each joint.

28. Place the back assembly, with attached side assemblies, on its back. Fit the bench assembly inside, with its bottom 14 inches from the lower ends of the verticals (A). Predrill holes for 3-inch lag bolts through the front verticals into the ends of the long bench supports (G). Insert the lag bolts and tighten them securely. Repeat this procedure to insert two more lag bolts through the verticals (A) into the ends of the other long bench supports (G).

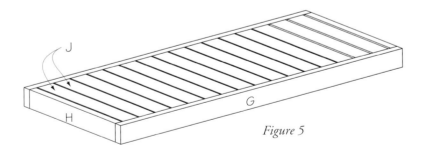

Figure 5

Making the Top

29. Cut two long top supports (K) from 2 x 4 pine, each measuring 64 inches long.

30. Cut two short top supports (L) from 2 x 4 pine, each measuring 24 inches long.

31. Place the two long top supports (K) on a level surface, parallel to each other and 24 inches apart, similar to the arrangement shown in figure 3 on page 72. Fit the two short top supports (L) between the two long top supports (K). Screw through the long top supports (K) into the ends of the short top supports (L), using two 2½-inch-long screws on each joint.

32. The top also contains a recessed lattice panel. To accommodate the panel, use a rabbet bit to rout the inner edges of one side of the top assembly, ¾ x ¾ inches.

33. Cut a top panel (M) from lattice, measuring 62½ x 25½ inches.

34. Fit the top panel (M) into the routed groove in the top assembly. Nail through the top panel (M) into the long top supports (K) and short top supports (L), using 1½-inch-long finishing nails.

35. Place the back assembly, with attached side and bench assemblies, on its back. Fit the top assembly inside, flush with the top edge of the verticals (A). Predrill holes for 3-inch lag bolts through the front verticals into the ends of the long top supports (K). Insert the lag bolts and tighten them securely. Repeat this procedure to insert two more lag bolts through the verticals (A) into the ends of the other long top supports (K).

Finishing

36. Cover any exposed edges of the lattice panels with leftover slats from the unused lattice panels. To secure them, use glue and 1½-inch-long nails spaced about every 5 inches.

37. Fill any cracks, crevices, or screw holes with wood filler, and thoroughly sand all surfaces of the completed project.

38. Seal and paint or stain your lattice bower the color of your choice.

PICKET WINDOW BOX

This pretty window box really comes alive when filled with colorful flowers. Not only does it look attractive mounted outside on a window ledge, but it also brightens up your window when admired from inside the house. The box is constructed around an inexpensive pre-made plastic planter. The size can be adjusted to fit any window.

Materials and Supplies

30 linear feet of 1 x 2 pine

2 linear feet of 2 x 2 pine

½ linear foot of 1 x 4 pine

Plastic planter box*

Hardware

150   3d x 1¼" nails

4   2" screws

Cutting List

Code	Description	Qty.	Materials	Dimensions
A	Long Supports	4	1 x 2 pine	29½" long
B	Short Supports	4	1 x 2 pine	7½" long
C	Pickets	23	1 x 2 pine	8" long
D	Posts	2	2 x 2 pine	8½" long
E	Post Cap	2	1 x 4 pine	2" x 2"

*Notes on Materials

We purchased a plastic planter box measuring 29 inches long, 5¼ inches deep, and 8¼ inches wide. It has a lip on the top that rests on the wooden supports we built. You can use this design for any size box you wish, but you need to adjust the dimensions accordingly. The support assemblies fit just under the top lip of the planter.

Constructing the Planter Supports

1. Cut four long supports (A) from 1 x 2 pine, each measuring 29½ inches long.

2. Cut four short supports (B) from 1 x 2 pine, each measuring 7½ inches long.

3. Place two long supports (A) on a level surface, parallel to each other and 7½ inches apart. Fit two short supports (B) between the long supports (A), as shown in figure 1. Nail through the long supports (A) into the ends of the short supports (B). Use two 1¼-inch-long nails on each joint.

Adding the Pickets

4. Cut 23 pickets (C) from 1 x 2 pine, each measuring 8 inches long.

5. Cut the corners off each of the 23 pickets (C), as shown in figure 2 on page 77.

6. Lay the two support assemblies on a level surface, parallel to each other, 1½ inches apart, with the long supports (A) on the top and bottom, and the short supports (B) on the sides. Attach all 15 pickets (C) to the top of both support assemblies, starting with the outer pickets, as shown in figure 3 on page 77. These outer pickets should be exactly flush with the ends of the long supports (A). Space the pickets ½ inch apart. Note that the square ends of the pickets are flush with the bottom edge of one long support (A), and the pointed end is 3½ inches higher than the top edge of the other long support (A). Apply

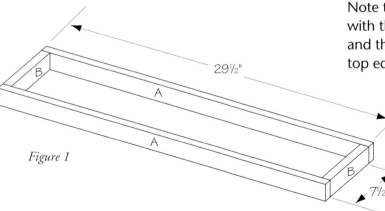

Figure 1

29½"

A

A

B

B

7½"

glue to the meeting surfaces, and nail through the pickets into both of the long supports (A), using two 1¼-inch long nails on each joint.

7. Follow the procedure in step 6 to attach four pickets to each of the short supports (B).

Adding the End Posts

8. Cut two posts (D) from 2 x 2 pine, each measuring 8½ inches long.

9. Cut two post caps (E) from 1 x 4 pine, each measuring 2 x 2 inches.

10. Center one post cap (E) over the end of one post (D). Apply glue to the meeting surfaces and nail through the post cap (E) into the end of the post (D), using two 1¼-inch-long nails. Repeat this procedure to attach the remaining post cap (E) to the second post (D).

11. Fit the posts on each end of the window box, filling in the exposed corner between the side and front pickets (C), as shown in figure 4. Screw through the inside corner of each of the support assemblies into the post (D), using a 2-inch-long screw on each joint.

Finishing

12. Fill any cracks, crevices, or screw holes with wood filler, and thoroughly sand all surfaces of the completed window box.

13. Seal and paint or stain your window box the color of your choice.

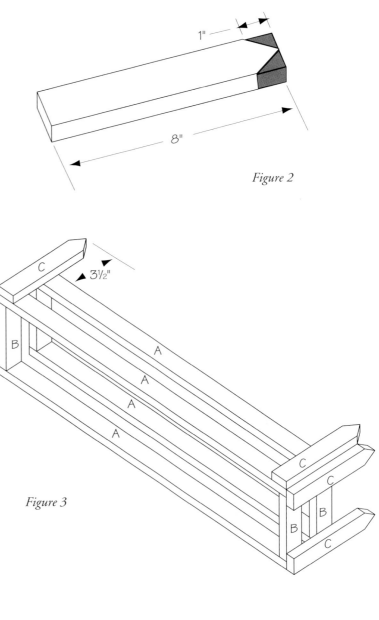

Figure 2

Figure 3

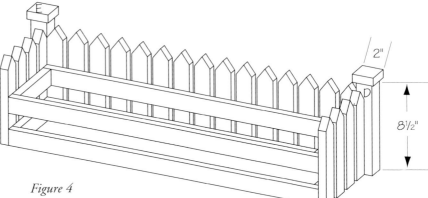

Figure 4

SIDE CHAIR

This handsome chair is comfortable, rugged enough for outdoor use, and very inexpensive to build. You might want to build four or more to go with the dining table shown on page 64, plus a few extra to keep in your garden, on the patio, or beside the jacuzzi.

Special Tools and Techniques

Dadoes

Miters

Materials and Supplies

10 linear feet of 2 x 4 pine

30 linear feet of 1"-thick pine, ripped to 2" in width (actual width after ripping will be ¾" x 2")

6 linear feet of 2"-thick pine, ripped to 2" in width (actual width after ripping will be 1½" x 2")

Hardware

20 3d x 1¼" nails

20 1¼" screws

6 3" screws

Cutting List

CODE	DESCRIPTION	QTY.	MATERIALS	DIMENSIONS
A	Back Leg	2	2 x 4 pine	37" long
B	Front Leg	2	2 x 4 pine	18" long
C	Front Rail	1	¾" x 2" ripped*	15½" long
D	Side Rail	2	¾" x 2" ripped	16" long
E	Back Rail	1	¾" x 2" ripped	15½" long
F	Side Spacer	2	¾" x 2" ripped	13½" long
G	Front Spacer	1	¾" x 2" ripped	14" long
H	Side Brace	2	1½" x 2" ripped	13½" long
I	Middle Brace	1	1½" x 2" ripped	14" long
J	Short Slat	1	¾" x 2" ripped	14" long
K	Long Slat	12	¾" x 2" ripped	18" long

*Note: All the ripped pieces are presented in actual dimensions.

Cutting the Legs

The back legs of the chair are cut from 2 x 4 pine. The chair legs are angled at the top to make the chair comfortable to sit in. Although it looks complicated, it's really simple to do. Just take your time and measure and cut correctly.

1. Cut two back legs (A) from 2 x 4 pine, each measuring 37 inches long.

2. Refer to figure 1 to mark and cut the first chair leg. Measure and mark points "a," "b," "c," and "d." Draw a line connecting "a" to "b,"

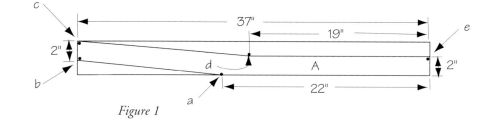

Figure 1

"c" to "d," and "d" to "e". Then cut along the lines to remove the shaded areas of the pattern. Use the resulting back leg (A) to cut a second back leg (A).

3. Measure 16 inches from what will be the bottom of the leg and cut a 2-inch-wide dado, ¾ inch deep in the leg (A), as shown in figure 2. Repeat this procedure to dado the remaining back leg (A). Because the dadoes will be on the inside of the chair back, the second dado must be a mirror image of the dado in the first back leg (A).

4. Cut two front legs (B) from 2 x 4 pine, each measuring 18 inches long. Rip each leg to a width of 2 inches.

5. The front legs (B) are dadoed to accept the seat rails. Follow figure 3 to dado the first front leg (B). Repeat this procedure to dado the second front leg (B). As with the back legs, the second front leg (B) must be the mirror image of the first front leg (B).

Adding the Chair Rails

6. Cut one front rail (C) from ¾-inch x 2-inch ripped pine, measuring 15½ inches long.

7. Miter both ends of the front rail (C) at opposing 45-degree angles, as shown in figure 4.

8. Cut two side rails (D) from ¾-inch x 2-inch ripped pine, each measuring 16 inches long. Miter one end of each of the side rails at opposing 45-degree angles, as shown in figure 5.

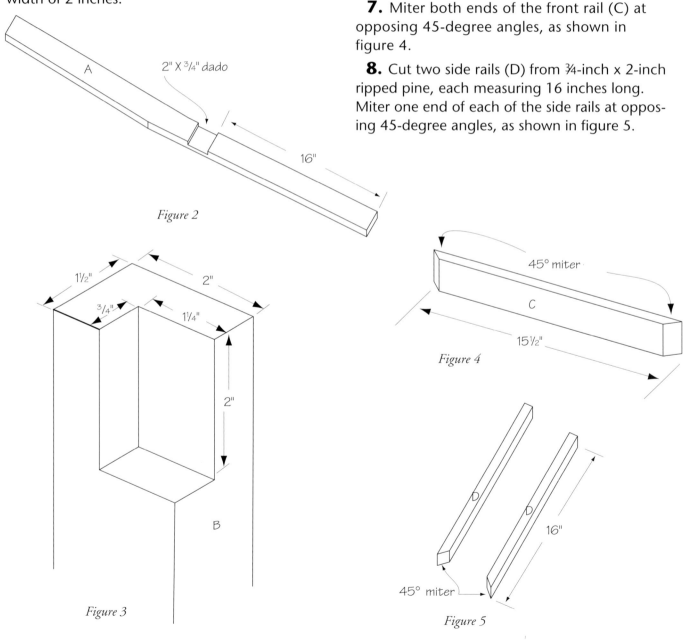

Figure 2

Figure 3

Figure 4

Figure 5

9. Cut one back rail (E) from ¾-inch x 2-inch ripped pine, measuring 15½ inches long.

10. Refer to figure 6 to connect the chair rails to the chair legs. First fit the unmitered ends of the side rails (D) into the dado in the back legs (A), ¾ inch from the back edge of the dado. Be sure that the miters in the side rails (D) face each other. Apply glue to the meeting surfaces and screw through the side rails (D) into the dado in the back leg (A), using two 1¼-inch-long screws on each joint.

11. Fit the back rail (E) over the unmitered ends of the side rails (D) inside the dadoes in each of the back legs (A). Apply glue to the meeting surfaces and screw through the back rail (E) into the ends of the side rails (D). Use two 1¼-inch-long screws on each joint.

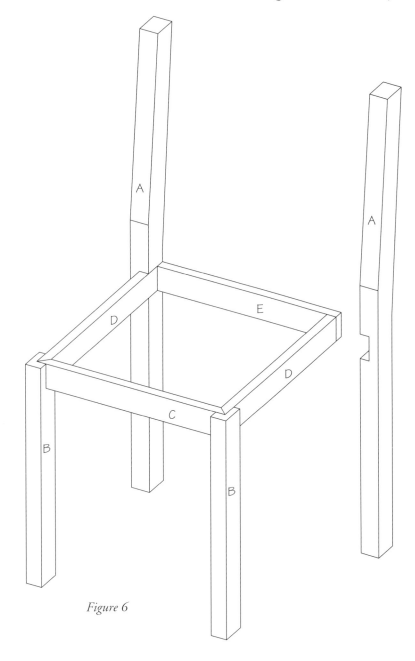

Figure 6

12. Fit the front rail (C) between the two mitered ends of the side rails (D) inside the dadoes in the front legs (B). Apply glue to the meeting surfaces and screw through the front rail (C) into the front legs (B). Use two 1¼-inch-long screws on each joint.

Adding the Spacers

13. Cut two side spacers (F) from ¾-inch x 2-inch ripped pine, each measuring 13½ inches long.

14. Fit one side spacer (F) face-to-face on the outside of the side rail (D), between the back leg (A) and the front leg (B), as shown in figure 7.

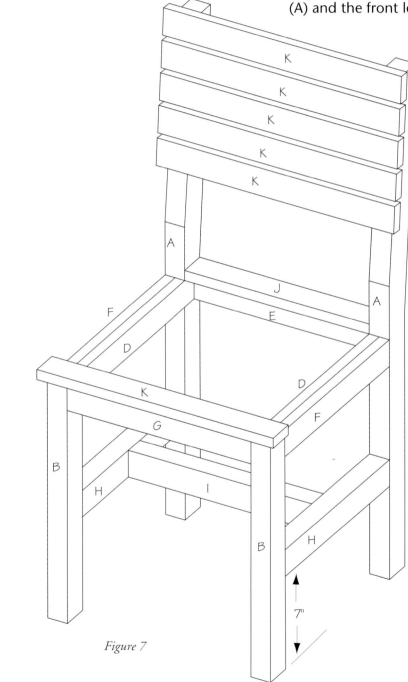

Figure 7

Apply glue to the meeting surfaces, and screw through the side rail (D) into the side spacer (F), using three 1¼-inch-long screws. Repeat this procedure to attach the remaining side spacer (F) to the opposite side rail (D).

15. Cut one front spacer (G) from ¾-inch x 2-inch ripped pine, measuring 14 inches long.

16. Fit the front spacer (G) face-to-face on the outside of the front rail (C), as shown in figure 7. Apply glue to the meeting surfaces and screw through the front rail (C) into the front spacer (G), using three 1¼-inch-long screws.

Adding the Leg Braces

17. Cut two side braces (H) from ½-inch x 2-inch ripped pine, each measuring 13½ inches long.

18. Fit one side brace (H) between a front leg (B) and back leg (A), 7 inches from the bottom of each of the legs, as shown in figure 7. Screw through the front and back legs (A and B) into the ends of the side braces (H), using a 3-inch-long screw on each joint. Repeat this procedure to attach the second side brace (H) between the remaining front and back legs (A and B).

19. Cut one middle brace (I) from 1½-inch x 2-inch ripped pine, measuring 14 inches long.

20. Center the middle brace (I) between the two side braces (H), as shown in figure 7. Screw through the side braces (H) into the ends of the middle brace (I), using a 3-inch-long screw.

Adding the Slats

21. Cut one short slat (J) from ¾-inch x 2-inch ripped pine, measuring 14 inches long.

22. Fit the short slat (J), wide surface up, on top of the back rail (E), between the two back legs (A), as shown in figure 7. Apply glue to the meeting surfaces and nail through the short slat (J) into the back rail (E), using three 1¼-inch nails.

23. Cut 12 long slats (K) from ¾-inch x 2-inch ripped pine, each measuring 18 inches long.

24. Seven long slats (K) will be used to complete the chair seat. Attach the first long slat (K) at the chair front, overhanging the front spacer (G) and each front leg (B) by ½ inch, as shown in figure 7. Apply glue to the meeting surfaces and nail through the long slat (K) into the front legs (B) and the front rail (C). Use two 1¼-inch-long nails on each front legs, and four 1¼-inch long nails on the front rail (C).

25. Attach the second long slat (K) at the back of the seat, ⅜ inch from the back legs (A) and overhanging the side spacers (F) by ½ inch. Apply glue to the meeting surfaces and nail through the long slat (K) into the side rails (D). Use two 1¼-inch-long nails on each joint.

26. Repeat the procedure in step 25 to attach five more long slats (K) to the chair seat, spacing them approximately ⅜ inch apart.

27. The remaining five long slats (K) are used for the chair back. Attach the first long slat ½ inch higher than the top of the back legs (A), with equal overlap on both side, as shown in figure 7. Nail through each long slat (K) into the back legs (A), using two 1¼-inch-long nails on each joint.

28. Attach the remaining four long slats (K) below the first one, about ⅜ inch apart, as shown in figure 7.

Finishing

29. Fill any cracks, crevices, or screw holes with wood filler, and thoroughly sand all surfaces of the completed chair.

30. Seal and paint or stain your chair the color of your choice.

OCCASIONAL TABLE

Small tables are always welcome in the garden or on the patio. This one is less than two feet square, so it will fit almost anywhere. Place one next to your favorite recliner, or make two of them and place them side by side to create a handy coffee table.

Special Tools and Techniques

Web clamps

Miters

Materials and Supplies

20 linear feet of 1 x 2 pine

15 linear feet of 1 x 4 pine

8 linear feet of 2 x 2 pine

2 linear feet of 2 x 4 pine

Hardware

40 4p x 1¼" nails

15 1¼" screws

30 1⅝" screws

10 2½" screws

4 4" screws

Cutting List

Code	Description	Qty.	Materials	Dimensions
A	Long Center Support	2	1 x 2 pine	14¾" long
B	Short Center Support	2	1 x 2 pine	13¼" long
C	Slat	8	1 x 2 pine	14¾" long
D	Trim	4	1 x 4 pine	21¾" long
E	Side	4	1 x 4 pine	14¾" long
F	Leg	4	2 x 2 pine	20" long
G	Triangular Support	4	2 x 4 pine	3½" long

Constructing the Table Top

1. Cut two long center supports (A) from 1 x 2 pine, each measuring 14¾ inches long.

2. Cut two short center supports (B) from 1 x 2 pine, each measuring 13¼ inches long.

3. Place the two short center supports (B) between the ends of the long center supports (A), as shown in figure 1. Screw through the long center supports (A) into the ends of the short center supports (B), using two 1⅝-inch-long screws on each joint.

4. Cut eight slats (C) from 1 x 2 pine, each measuring 14¾ inches long.

5. Place the eight slats (C) over the assembled center supports, as shown in figure 2. Space the slats (C) evenly across the width of the supports, leaving a little less than ¼ inch between slats and the same amount on both sides, as shown in figure 2. The exact measurement is not critical—just make certain that all the spaces are equal and that the slats (C) are all straight. Nail through the ends of the slats (C) into the long center supports (A), using two 1¼-inch-long nails on each end.

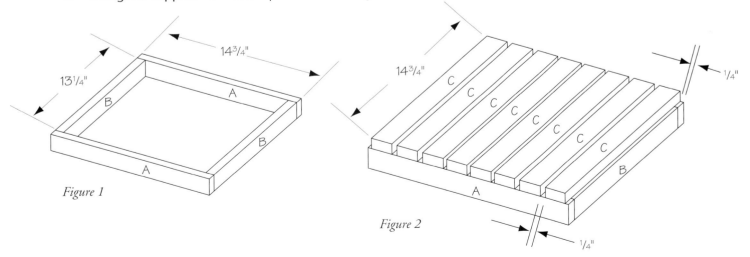

Figure 1

Figure 2

6. Cut four sides (E) from 1 x 4 pine, each measuring 14¾ inches.

7. Attach the four sides (E) to the long and short center supports (B and C), as shown in figure 3, even with the corners of the box made with the center supports in step 3. The open corners will later accommodate the legs for the table. Apply glue to the meeting surfaces, and screw through the supports (A and B) into the four sides (E). Use three 1¼-inch screws to secure each side (E).

8. The next step is to frame the slat assembly with the trim pieces (D). Cut four trims (D) from 1 x 4 pine, each measuring 21¾ inches long. Miter both ends of all four trim pieces at opposing 45-degree angles, as shown in figure 4. The long edge of each trim (D) should measure 21-¾ inches and the short edge should measure 14¾ inches.

9. Glue and clamp together the four trims (D) to form a four-sided picture frame. A web clamp is useful for this maneuver. Let the assembly dry overnight.

10. Position the assembled trim frame over the sides (E) around the slat assembly, as shown in figure 5. It should be placed even with the inside edges of the four sides (E). Apply glue to the meeting surfaces, and nail through each of the trims (D) into the sides (E). Use four or five 1⅝-inch-long nails on each trim piece (D).

Adding the Legs

11. Cut four legs (F) from 2 x 2 pine, each measuring 20 inches long.

12. Cut four triangular supports (G) at a 45-degree angle from 2 x 4 pine so that the grain runs with the long sides, as shown in figure 6 on page 87.

13. Predrill a ½-inch-diameter hole to a depth of 1 inch, beginning at the center of the long side of the triangular support (G) toward the 45-degree corner, as shown in figure 6.

14. Turn the assembled top upside down on a level surface. Apply glue to the short sides of the triangular supports (G), and place them in each

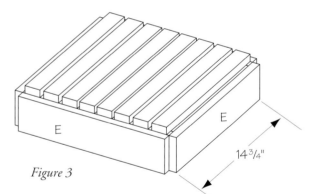

Figure 3

14³/₄"

45° miter

21³/₄"

Figure 4

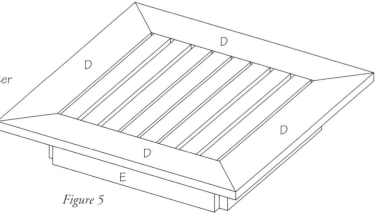

Figure 5

of the four inside corners formed by the sides (E), on top of the top supports (A and B), as shown in figure 7. Screw through the ends of the triangular supports (G) into the top supports (A and B) and the sides (E). Use two 1⅝-inch-long screws on each support.

15. Position each of the four legs (F) at the corners of the assembly, between the ends of the sides (E), as shown in figure 7. Make very certain that the legs are square to the assembly. Then insert a 4-inch-long screw into the predrilled hole in each triangular support (G), and screw it through the triangular support (G) and into each leg (F).

16. To further support the legs (F), carefully turn the entire assembly upside down. Again check to make certain that the legs are perfectly

square and straight. Then screw through each of the trim pieces (D) down into the leg (F). Use two 2½-inch-long screws on each leg (F)—one through each trim piece (D).

Finishing

17. If you want a very finished look, fill any cracks, crevices, or screw holes with wood filler, and thoroughly sand all surfaces of the occasional table.

18. You can seal and paint or stain the completed occasional table the color of your choice, or—if you used treated lumber—simply leave it natural, as shown in the photograph on page 84.

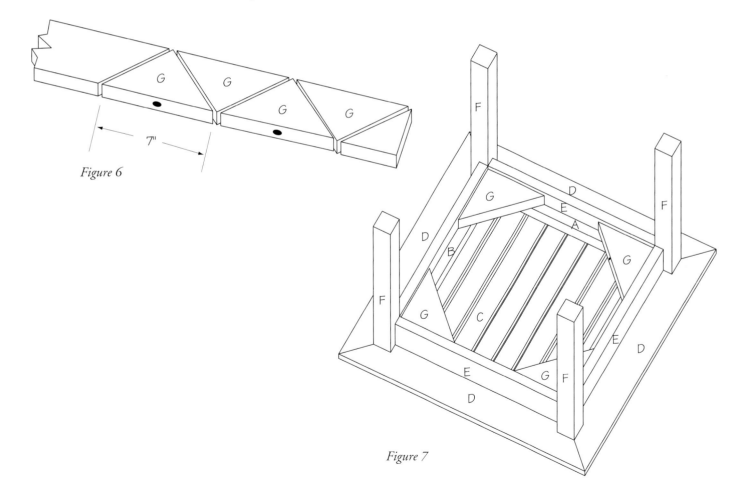

Figure 6

Figure 7

VICTORIAN LOVESEAT

Looks are deceiving in the case of this romantic loveseat. Although the piece looks difficult to make, the Victorian touches are gingerbread wooden brackets that can be purchased in most building-supply stores. By the time you sand and finish the loveseat, friends will assume it was built by a master woodworker!

Special Tools and Techniques

Dadoes

Bar clamps

Materials and Supplies

40 linear feet of 2 x 4 pine

15 linear feet of 1 x 4 pine

12 linear feet of 1 x 2 pine

1 piece of ½"-thick exterior plywood, measuring 20¼" x 46"

2 decorative gingerbread brackets, each measuring 8" x 12" on the straight sides*

2 decorative gingerbread brackets, each measuring 6" x 8½" on the straight sides*

Hardware

125	3d x 1¼" nails
80	4d x 1½" nails
20	3½" screws
15	2½" screws

Cutting List

CODE	DESCRIPTION	QTY.	MATERIALS	DIMENSIONS
A	Side Slat	6	1 x 4 pine	14" long
B	Horizontal Side	4	2 x 4 pine	15½" long
C	Vertical Sides	4	2 x 4 pine	34" long
D	Outer Seat Support	2	2 x 4 pine	45½" long
E	Center Seat Support	1	2 x 4 pine	19½" long
F	Short Inner Support	2	1 x 2 pine	19½" long
G	Long Inner Support	4	1 x 2 pine	20¼" long
H	Seat	1	½" plywood	19½" x 45½"
I	Horizontal Back	2	2 x 4 pine	45½" long
J	Back Slat	8	1 x 4 pine	10¼" long
K	Center Trim	1	2 x 4 pine	8" long*
L	Large Bracket	2		8" x 12"
M	Small Bracket	2		6" x 8½"

*Notes on Materials

It's not a necessity to find the exact decorative brackets that we used. Any design will work, but the size of the large brackets should be approximately the same as specified. If they are slightly different, you will need to alter the length of the center trim piece (K) to match the measurement of your bracket.

Constructing the Bench Sides

1. Cut six side slats (A) from 1 x 4 pine, each measuring 14 inches long.

2. Cut four horizontal sides (B) from 2 x 4 pine, each measuring 15½ inches long.

3. Cut a ¾-inch-wide dado, ½ inch deep, down the length of one edge of each of the horizontal sides (B), as shown in figure 1.

4. Working on a level surface, place two horizontal sides (B) parallel to each other, with the dadoes to the inside, as shown in figure 2. Fit the ends of three side slats (A) into the dadoes in each of the two horizontal sides (B). When the side slats (A) are properly fitted into the dadoes, the distance between the two horizontal sides (B) should measure 13 inches, as shown in figure 2. The two outer side slats (A) should be even with the ends of the horizontal sides (B), and 2½ inches from the center side slat (A). When the position is perfect, the overall measurements of the slat assembly should be 20 inches high and 15½ inches wide. Secure the slats in place by nailing through the dadoed edge of the horizontal sides (B) into the ends of the side slats (A), using two 1¼-inch-long nails on each joint.

5. Cut four vertical sides (C) from 2 x 4 pine, each measuring 34 inches long.

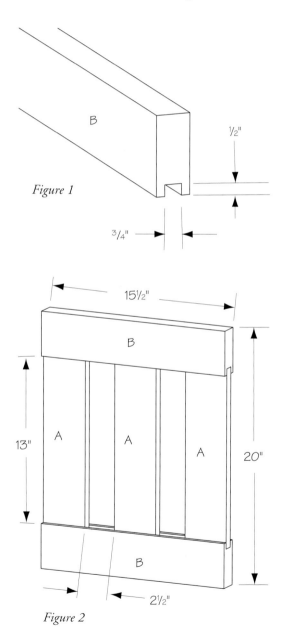

Figure 1

Figure 2

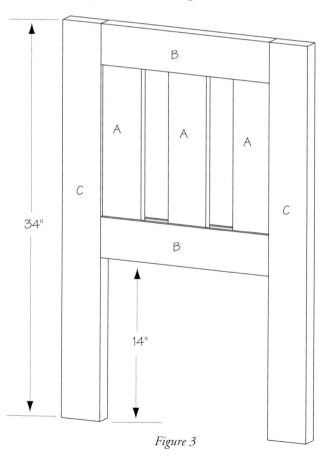

Figure 3

6. Place the slat assembly between two vertical sides (C), so that the top edge of the slat assembly is even with one end of the vertical sides (C), and is 14 inches from the other end of that same vertical side (C), as shown in figure 3 on page 90. Toenail through the edges of the horizontal sides (B) into the vertical sides (C), using a 3½-inch-long nail on each joint.

7. Repeat steps 3 through 6 to assemble the second side.

Adding the Seat

8. Cut two outer seat supports (D) from 2 x 4 pine, each measuring 45½ inches long.

9. For the next step, you may want to ask a helper to assist. If you are working alone, use a bar clamp to hold the assembly while you screw it together. Place the side assemblies (C) on one 34-inch-long edge, parallel to each other, 45½ inches apart, as shown in figure 4. Fit one outer seat support (D) between the two side assemblies, 16½ inches down from the upper edge of the two side assemblies. The top edge of the outer seat support (D) should be exactly even with the top edge of the lower horizontal side (B). Screw through the side assemblies into the ends of the outer seat support (D), using two 2½-inch-long screws on each joint.

10. Turn the assembly upside down, and attach the remaining outer seat support (D) to the opposite side of the side assemblies in the same manner you used in step 9.

11. Cut one center seat support (E) from 2 x 4 pine, measuring 19½ inches long.

12. Fit the center seat support (E) in the center of the assembly (wide surface up), between the outer seat supports (D), as

shown in figure 5. The center seat support (E) should be placed ½ inch below the top of the outer seat supports (D), centered between the side assemblies. Screw through the outer seat supports (D) into the ends of the center seat support (E). Use two 2½-inch-long screws on each of the joints.

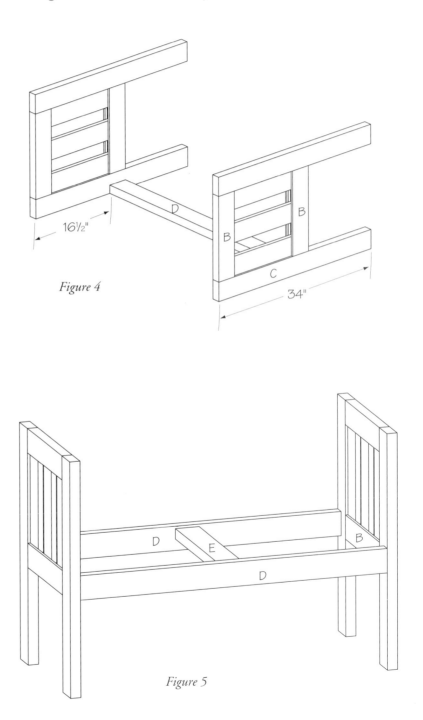

Figure 4

Figure 5

Adding the Inner Supports

13. Cut two short inner supports (F) from 1 x 2 pine, each measuring 19½ inches long.

14. Attach one short inner support (F) to the lower horizontal side (B), between the two outer seat supports (D), ½ inch below the top edge of the lower horizontal sides (B), as shown in figure 6. Apply glue to the meeting surfaces, and nail through the short inner support (F) into the lower horizontal side (A). Use three 1½-inch-long nails to secure it in place.

15. Repeat step 14 to attach the remaining short inner support (F) to the opposite lower horizontal side (A).

16. Cut four long inner supports (G) from 1 x 2 pine, each measuring 20¼ inches long.

17. Attach one long inner support (G) to the inner surface of the outer seat supports (D), ½ inch below the top edge of the outer seat supports (D), between the one short inner support

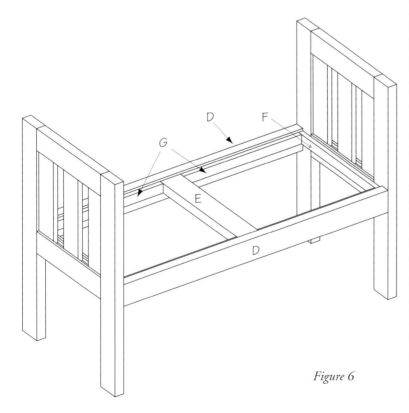

Figure 6

(F) and the center seat support (E), as shown in figure 6. Apply glue to the meeting surfaces, and use four 1½-inch-long nails spaced evenly along the length to secure it in place.

18. Repeat step 17 three more times to attach the remaining long inner supports (G) to the inside of the other outer seat supports (D).

19. Cut one seat (H) from ½-inch plywood, measuring 19½ x 45½ inches.

20. Place the seat (H) over the inner supports (F and G) and the center support (E). Apply glue to the meeting surfaces, and nail through the seat (H) into the center seat support (E) and into the inner seat supports (F and G). Use 1¼-inch-long nails spaced about every 4 or 5 inches.

Constructing the Loveseat Back

21. Cut two horizontal backs (I) from 2 x 4 pine, each measuring 45½ inches long.

22. Cut a ¾-inch-wide dado, ½ inch deep down the length of one edge of each of the horizontal backs (I), in the same manner as shown in figure 1 on page 90.

23. Cut eight back slats (J) from 1 x 4 pine, each measuring 10¼ inches long.

24. Working on a level surface, place the horizontal backs (I) parallel to each other, with the dadoes to the inside, in the same manner as shown in figure 2 on page 90. Fit the ends of the eight back slats (J) into the dadoes in each of the two horizontal backs (I). When the back slats (E) are properly fitted into the dadoes, the distance between the two horizontal backs (I) should measure 9¼ inches. The two outer back slats (E) should be even with the ends of the horizontal backs (I) and 2½ inches from each other, in the same manner as shown in figure 3 on page 90. When the position is perfect, the overall measurements of the back assembly should be 16¼ inches high and 45½ inches wide. Secure the slats by nailing through the dadoed edge of the horizontal backs (I) into the ends of the back slats (J), using two 1¼-inch-long nails on each joint.

25. Now you are ready to fit the back assembly between the two sides. To make the loveseat more comfortable, the back assembly is tilted at an angle—out at the top and in at the bottom. The tilt angle is determined by the width of the 2 x 4 on the side assemblies. The lower edge of the back is fitted flush with the inside edge of the vertical sides (C), and the upper edge of the back is fitted flush with the outer edge of the vertical sides (C), as shown in figure 7. When you have the back fitted perfectly, secure the assembly with bar clamps. Screw through the vertical sides (C) into the ends of the horizontal backs (I), using two 3½-inch-long screws on each joint.

Adding the Decorative Trim

26. Cut one center trim (K) from 2 x 4 pine, measuring 8 inches long. (Note: You will need to adjust this measurement if the gingerbread corner pieces you purchased differ in height from those specified in the materials list.)

27. Attach one large wooden bracket (L) to the 8-inch edge of the center trim (K), using the photograph on page 94 as a guide. Appy glue to the meeting edges, and toenail though the sides and the ends of the large bracket (L) into the edge of the center trim (K). Use three 1½-inch-long nails on each side, and one nail on each end. Repeat this procedure to attach the other large bracket.

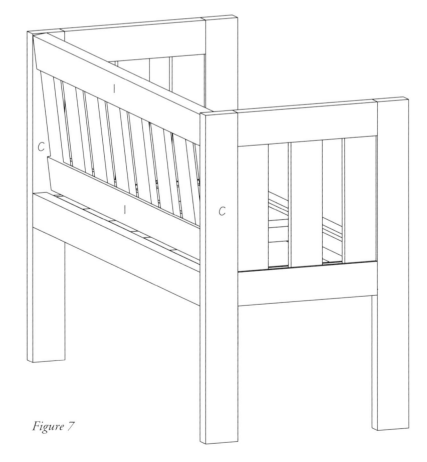

Figure 7

28. Measure carefully to find the center of the back assembly and the center of the trim assembly. Matching those two points, apply glue to the meeting surfaces, attach the trim assembly to the top back center of the bench. Toenail through the brackets into the top back of the bench, using 1½-inch-long nails.

29. Attach the smaller wooden brackets (M) to the loveseat in the same manner, flush with the inside corner formed by the front edges of the vertical sides (C) and the outer seat supports (D), using the photograph below as a guide. The 8½-inch-long side of the small bracket should be against the outer seat supports (D).

Finishing

30. Fill any cracks, crevices, or screw holes with wood filler, and thoroughly sand all surfaces of the completed loveseat.

31. Seal and paint or stain your Victorian loveseat the color of your choice.

A word of caution: Because the gingerbread trim pieces are fragile, never attempt to move the finished loveseat by holding onto the trim pieces, as they will most likely break.

RECTANGULAR PLANTER

This good-looking planter measures 18 x 20 inches, and will accommodate very large plants. It's also a quick-and-easy project to build. If you have ever priced large planter boxes in a garden store, then you will really appreciate how economical this one is to make.

Materials and Supplies

14 linear feet of 1 x 2 pine

8 linear feet of 1 x 4 pine

28 linear feet of 1 x 6 pine

1 piece of ½"-thick exterior plywood, measuring 16½" x 20½"

Hardware

120 1¼" screws

Cutting List

CODE	DESCRIPTION	QTY.	MATERIALS	DIMENSIONS
A	Long Inner Support	4	1 x 2 pine	20½" long
B	Short Inner Support	4	1 x 2 pine	15" long
C	Bottom	1	½" plywood	16½" x 20½"
D	Side Panel	14	1 x 6 pine	18" long
E	Short Trim	2	1 x 4 pine	19" long
F	Long Trim	2	1 x 4 pine	22" long

Making the Inner Supports

1. Cut four long inner supports (A) from 1 x 2 pine, each measuring 20½ inches long.

2. Cut four short inner support (B) from 1 x 2 pine, each measuring 15 inches long.

3. Place two long inner supports (A) parallel to each other and 15 inches apart. Fit two short inner supports (B) between the ends of the long inner supports (A), as shown in figure 1. Screw through the ends of the long inner supports (A) into the short inner supports (B), using two 1¼-inch-long screws on each of the joints.

4. Repeat step 3 to form a second assembly using the remaining two long inner supports (A) and two short inner supports (B).

Adding the Bottom

5. Cut one bottom (C) from ½-inch-thick plywood, measuring 16½ x 20½ inches.

6. Drill six 1-inch holes through the bottom (C) to allow for drainage. The exact placement is not critical, but they should be well distributed across the bottom (C).

7. Attach the bottom (C) to one inner assembly, as shown in figure 1. Apply glue to the meeting surfaces, and screw through the bottom (C) into the edges of the long inner supports (A) and short inner supports (B).

Adding the Sides

8. Cut 14 side panels (D) from 1 x 6 pine, each measuring 18 inches long.

9. Working on a level surface, place three side panels (D) next to each other, wide sides up. Place one 16½-inch-long side of the inner support assembly—with bottom (C) attached—¾ inch from one end of the three panels, as shown in figure 2. Apply glue to the meeting surfaces, and screw through the short inner supports (B) into each of the three side panels (D). Use two 1¼-inch-long screws on each of the side panels (D). Repeat this process to attach the other support assembly to the same three side panels (D), flush with the opposite ends of the side panels (D).

10. Repeat step 9 to attach three side panels (D) to the opposite side of the two support assemblies, as shown in figure 3 on page 97.

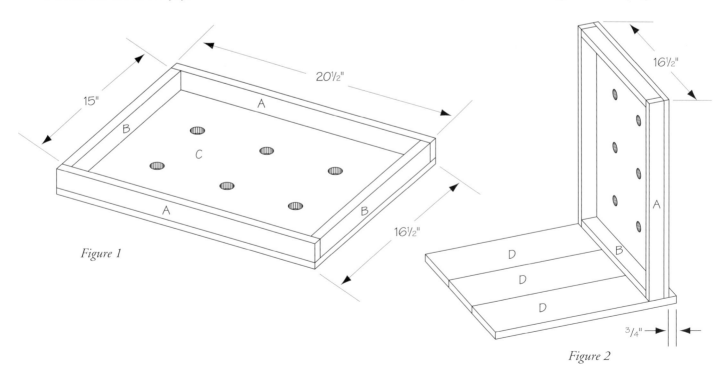

15"

20½"

A

B

C

A

B

16½"

16½"

A

D

B

D

D

¾"

Figure 1

Figure 2

11. Repeat step 9 to attach four side panels (D) to one long side of the two support assemblies, as shown in figure 3. Note that these four side panels (D) will overlap the three side panels (D) that you previously attached.

12. Repeat step 11 to attach the remaining four side panels (D) to the remaining long side of the two support assemblies.

Adding the Trim

13. Cut two short trims (E) from 1 x 4 pine, each measuring 19 inches long.

14. Cut two long trims (F) from 1 x 4 pine, each measuring 22 inches long.

15. As shown in figure 4, position the short trims (E) so that their inside edges are flush with the inside faces of the long inner supports (A). The ends of the short trims (E) must be even with the inside edges of the short inner supports (B). The trims will overlap the planter by 2 inches. Apply glue to the top edge of each long

inner support (A) and each side panel (D); then screw through each short trim (E) into the long inner support (A), using four 1¼-inch-long screws for each trim.

16. Position each long trim (F) with its inside edge flush with the inside face of a short inner support (B) and its ends even with the outside edges of the short trims (E), as shown in figure 4. Apply glue to the top edge of each short inner support (B) and each side panel (D); then screw through each long trim (F) into the short inner support (B), using four 1¼-inch-long screws for each trim.

Finishing

17. We left our planter unfinished, but if you wish a more formal look, fill any cracks, crevices, or screw holes with wood filler, and thoroughly sand all surfaces of the completed planter.

18. Paint or stain the finished project the color of your choice, or simply seal it with a water-proof sealer for a natural look.

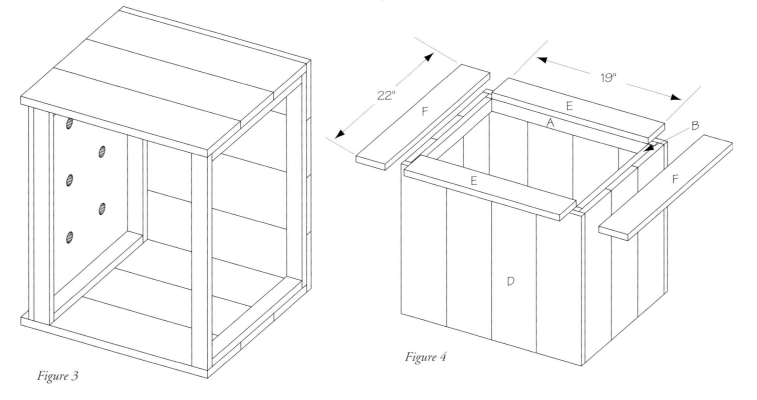

Figure 3

Figure 4

POTTING BENCH

This simple pine potting bench is a great help to any gardener. The bottom shelf can store large gardening items that take up space in the garage, and the top shelves can accommodate small pots, insecticides, and other necessaries. There is also a drawer for stowing gardening tools. The work surface features a drop-in container to hold potting soil. With this handy potting bench on your side, we bet your garden will be the prettiest in the neighborhood!

Special Tools and Techniques

Bar clamps

Mitering

Materials and Supplies

32 linear feet of 1 x 8 pine

12 linear feet of 1 x 6 pine

45 linear feet of 1 x 4 pine

10 linear feet of 1 x 2 pine

4 linear feet of 1 x 1 pine

25 linear feet of 2 x 4 pine

1 piece of ⅜"-thick exterior plywood, measuring 2' x 2'

Heavy-duty plastic dishpan, approximately 11" x 13"

Hardware

20 2½" screws

50 1⅝" screws

50 1½" screws

35 1¼" screws

10 4d x 1½" nails

20 3d x 1¼" nails

35 2d x 1" nails

Cutting List

Code	Description	Qty.	Materials	Dimensions
A	Horizontal Sides	4	2 x 4 pine	20½" long
B	Vertical Sides	4	2 x 4 pine	33" long
C	Side Trim	2	1 x 4 pine	23½" long
D	Long Trim	1	1 x 4 pine	52½" long
E	Shelf Slat	4	1 x 4 pine	51" long
F	Wide Top	2	1 x 8 pine	60½" long
G	Narrow Top	2	1 x 6 pine	60½" long
H	Edge Support	2	1 x 2 pine	20" long
I	Reinforcements	2	1 x 2 pine	14" long
J	Shelf Sides	2	1 x 8 pine	34" long
K	Shelf Back	2	1 x 4 pine	59" long
L	Shelf	2	1 x 8 pine	59" long
M	Bottom Support	1	2 x 4 pine	59" long
N	Drawer Side	2	⅜" plywood	5" x 6⅞"
O	Drawer Glides	2	1 x 1 pine	7¼" long
P	Drawer Bottom	1	⅜" plywood	14½" x 6⅞"
Q	Drawer Back	1	⅜" plywood	15½" x 5"
R	Drawer Front	1	1 x 8 pine	18¾" long
S	Horizontal Drawer Support	1	1 x 2 pine	22" long
T	Vertical Drawer Support	1	1 x 1 pine	22" long
U	Top Support	2	2 x 4 pine	8" long

Constructing the Side Supports

1. Cut four horizontal sides (A) from 2 x 4 pine, each measuring 20½ inches long.

2. Cut four vertical sides (B) from 2 x 4 pine, each measuring 33 inches long.

3. To form the side supports, place two vertical sides (B) parallel to each other and 20½ inches apart. Fit two horizontal sides (A) between the two vertical sides (B), as shown in figure 1. The uppermost horizontal side (A) should be even with the top ends of both vertical sides (B), and the lower horizontal side (A) should be 6½ inches from the lower ends of both vertical sides (B). Screw through the vertical sides (B) into the ends of the horizontal sides (A). Use two 2½-inch-long screws on each of the joints. Repeat this procedure to form a second side support, using the remaining two vertical sides (B) and horizontal sides (A).

Adding the Trim

4. Cut two side trims (C) from 1 x 4 pine, each measuring 23½ inches long.

5. Apply glue to the meeting surfaces, and attach one side trim piece (C) to the top of one assembled side support, as shown in figure 2. Screw through the side trim (C) into the upper horizontal side (A) and the two vertical sides (B). Use two 1⅝-inch-long screws on each of the vertical sides (B) and three screws on the horizontal sides (A). Repeat this procedure to attach the remaining side trim (C) to the other assembled side support.

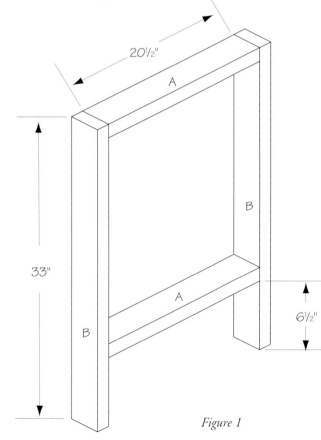

Figure 1

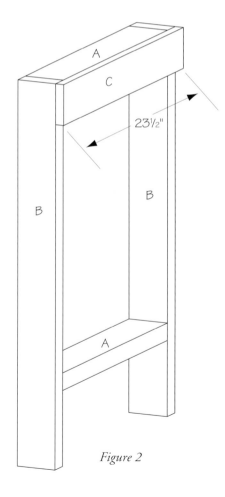

Figure 2

6. Cut one long trim (D) from 1 x 4 pine, measuring 52½ inches long.

7. Place the two side supports on a level surface, parallel to each other and 44 inches apart, with the side trim (C) on the outside. Fit the long trim (D) over the exposed ends of the side trim (C), as shown in figure 3. Screw through the long trim (D) into the vertical sides (B). Use two 1⅝-inch-long screws on each joint.

8. Cut four shelf slats (E) from 1 x 4 pine, each measuring 51 inches long.

9. Position the shelf slats (E) evenly spaced over each of the lower horizontal sides (A), as shown in figure 3. Screw through the ends of the shelf slats (E) into the top of the lower horizontal sides (A), using two 1⅝-inch-long screws on each joint.

Making the Work Surface

10. Cut two wide tops (F) from 1 x 8 pine, each measuring 60½ inches long.

11. Cut two narrow tops (G) from 1 x 6 pine, each measuring 60½ inches long.

12. Place the four tops (F and G) parallel to each other, with the wide tops (F) on the outside and the narrow tops (G) on the inside to form a rectangle measuring 25½ x 60½ inches, as shown in figure 4. Apply glue to the meeting surfaces and clamp the tops together, making certain that all four tops are level along their entire length. Allow the boards to set up overnight.

13. Cut two edge supports (H) from 1 x 2 pine, each measuring 20 inches long. These will be used to reinforce the glued top. Screw them to the rectangular top, positioning them 2¾ inches from the front and back, and 2 inches from the sides, as shown in figure 5. Use eight 1¼-inch-long screws on each edge support (H).

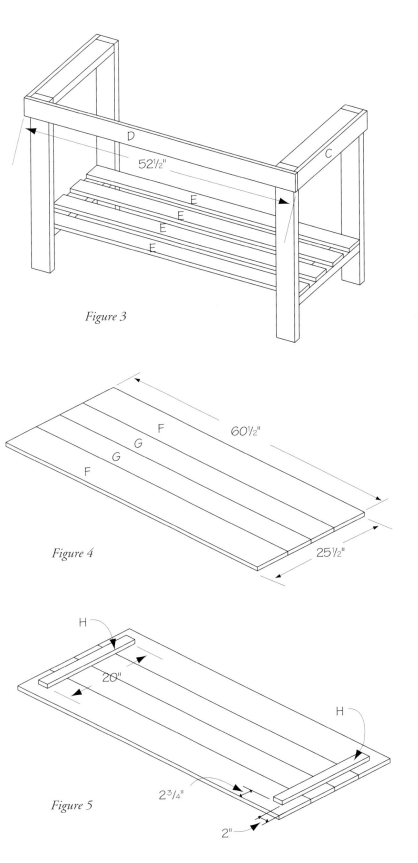

Figure 3

Figure 4

Figure 5

Adding the Potting Bin

14. The next step is to cut a hole in the rectangular top to accommodate the potting bin. We used a heavy-duty plastic dishpan for our bin. With the rectangular top upside down, and the edge supports (H) showing, turn the dishpan upside down in the position shown in figure 6. Holding the dishpan in that position, trace around it with a pencil to transfer the outline to the wood surface. Remove the dishpan. Draw an inner outline about ½ inch smaller, which will be the true cutting line. This will allow the dishpan to drop through the hole, with the dishpan lip resting on the wood. Make certain that all four sides of your hole are parallel to the four sides of the rectangular top. When you are satisfied that the position and size of the hole are correct, cut out the center section to accommodate the dishpan.

15. To reinforce the top around the edge of the hole, cut two reinforcements (I) from 1 x 2 pine, each measuring 14 inches long.

16. Place the two reinforcements (I) flush with the long edges of the hole, with an equal length of the reinforcement (I) extending past the hole, as shown in figure 6. Screw through the reinforcements (I) into the rectangular top, using six 1¼-inch-long screws on each reinforcement (I).

17. Turn the rectangular top right side up. Center it on top of the side suports. The top should overhang the side supports 4 inches at the sides and 1½ inches at the back.

18. Attach the rectangular top to the side supports. Screw through the top into each of the side supports using five 1⅝-inch-long screws spaced evenly along the joint.

Making the Upper Shelf Section

19. Cut two shelf sides (J) from 1 x 8 pine, each measuring 34 inches long.

20. Cut two shelf backs (K) from 1 x 4 pine, each measuring 59 inches long.

21. Cut two shelves (L) from 1 x 8 pine, each measuring 59 inches long.

22. Glue one shelf (L) to the edge of one shelf back (K), aligning the bottoms of the two pieces, as shown in figure 7. Reinforce the joint by driving 1⅝-inch-long screws every 6 inches. Repeat this step to join the other shelf (L) and shelf back (K).

23. Place the two shelf sides (J) on a level surface, parallel to each other, and 59 inches apart. Fit one shelf/back assembly between the two shelf sides (J), flush with the ends of both shelf

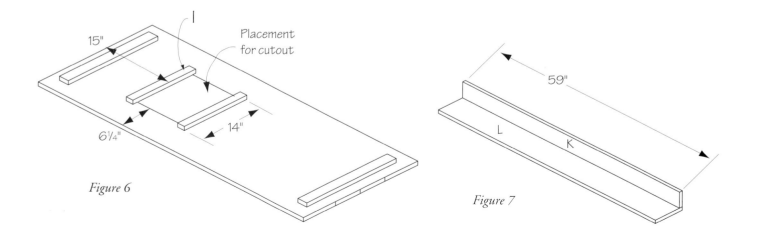

15"

I

Placement for cutout

6¼"

14"

Figure 6

59"

L

K

Figure 7

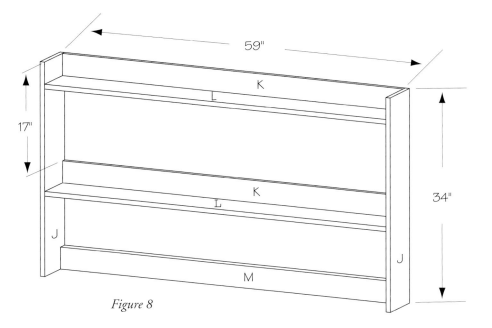

Figure 8

sides (J), as shown in figure 8. Screw through the shelf sides (J) in the ends of the shelf back (K) and the shelf (L). Use two 1⅝-inch-long screws in each end of the shelf back (K) and three screws in each end of the shelf (L).

24. Repeat step 23 to attach the remaining shelf/back assembly between the two shelf sides (J), 17 inches from the top of the shelf sides (J), as shown in figure 8.

25. Cut one bottom support (M) from 2 x 4 pine, measuring 59 inches long.

26. Attach the bottom support (M) between the two shelf sides (J), flush with the lower ends of the shelf sides (J), as shown in figure 8. Screw through the shelf sides (J) into the ends of the bottom support (M), using two 2½-inch-long screws on each of the joints.

Adding the Drawer

27. Cut two drawer sides (N) from ⅜-inch exterior plywood, each measuring 5 x 6⅞ inches.

28. Cut two drawer glides (O) from 1 x 1 pine, each 7¼ inches long. To allow the drawers to slide without binding, plane or rip the

drawer slides (O) on one side so they measure 1¹⁄₁₆ x ¾ inch.

29. Apply glue to the meeting surfaces, and attach one drawer glide (O) to one 6⅞-inch edge of a drawer side (N), using three 1-inch-long finishing nails, as shown in figure 9. Note that the drawer glide (O) extends past the drawer side (N) by ⅜ inch on one end.

30. Repeat step 29 to attach the remaining drawer glide (O) to the other drawer side (N). The ⅜-inch extension should be a mirror image of the one in step 29.

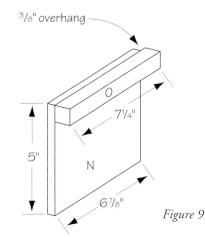

Figure 9

31. Cut one drawer bottom (P) from ⅜-inch exterior plywood, measuring 14½ x 6⅞ inches.

32. Cut one drawer back (Q) from ⅜-inch exterior plywood, measuring 15¼ x 5 inches.

33. Assemble the drawer bottom (P), drawer sides (N), and drawer back (Q), as shown in figure 10, fitting the drawer back (Q) over the ends of the sides (N), and the drawer bottom (P) flush with the bottom edges of the drawer sides (N). Nail through the drawer sides (N) and drawer back (Q) into the edges of the drawer bottom (P). Use 1-inch-long finishing nails spaced about 3 inches apart.

34. Cut one drawer front (R) from 1 x 8 pine, measuring 18¾ inches long.

35. Rout the edges of the drawer front (R) with a round-over bit (optional) or simply sand the edges to slightly round them.

36. Attach the drawer front (R) to the drawer assembly. Center the drawer front (R) so that it is ¾ inch above the drawer assembly at the top and extends 1 inch beyond each of the drawer glides (O), as shown in figure 10. Nail through the drawer front into the ends of the drawer

sides (N), drawer bottoms (P), and drawer glides (O), using 1½-inch long finishing nails. Use two nails on each joint.

Adding the Drawer Supports

37. The drawer supports are comprised of two pieces of wood glued together. We will assemble the two pieces first, and cut the resulting assembly to form two supports. Cut one horizontal drawer support (S) from 1 x 2 pine, measuring 22 inches long.

38. Cut one vertical drawer support (T) from 1 x 1 pine, measuring 22 inches long.

39. Apply glue to the meeting surfaces, and attach the vertical drawer support (T) to one edge of the horizontal support (S), as shown in figure 11. Align the long edges accurately. Use 1¼-inch finishing nails, spacing them every 3 or 4 inches. Allow the glue to set up.

40. Cut two drawer supports from the glued support assembly, each measuring 7¼ inches long.

41. Mount one drawer support under the lower shelf (L), ½ inch from the right shelf side (J), as shown in figure 12 on page 105. Screw through the top of the shelf (L) into the drawer support, using two 1¼-inch-long screws.

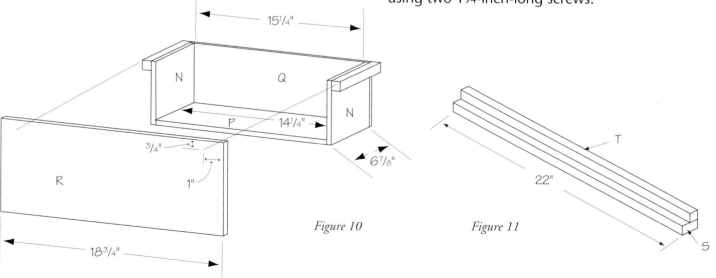

Figure 10

Figure 11

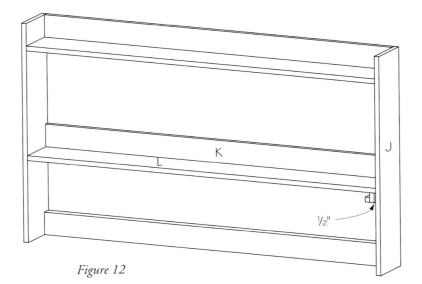

Figure 12

42. Slide the drawer in place, and mark the placement of the second drawer support. Be sure to leave a little play in your measurements—you don't want to have to force the drawer open and closed. Attach the second drawer support under the lower shelf following your placement marks.

Attaching the Top Shelf Section

43. Cut two top supports (U) from 2 x 4 pine, each measuring 8 inches long.

44. Miter one end of each of the two top supports (U) at a 45-degree angle, as shown in figure 13.

45. Apply glue to the meeting surfaces and attach the top supports to the back of the side supports on the lower section, against the

rectangular top. Screw through the top supports (U) into the ends of the horizontal sides (A) and the edges of the vertical sides (B). Use two 2½-inch-long screws on each joint.

46. Place the top shelf assembly over the bottom assembly, matching the sides and backs. To make the potting bench portable, we skipped the glue; that way, the two sections can be separated for transporting. Screw through the bench top (from underneath) into the bottom ends of the shelf sides (J). Use three 1⅝-inch-long screws on each joint.

Finishing

47. We used a 6-inch-length of the remaining support assembly to fashion our drawer pull, and screwed it to the front of the drawer front using two 1⅝-inch-long screws. You can use the same technique, or purchase a different drawer pull at the hardware store.

48. Fill any cracks, crevices, or screw holes with wood filler, and thoroughly sand all surfaces of the completed potting bench.

49. It is a good idea to seal the completed bench with an exterior grade sealer.

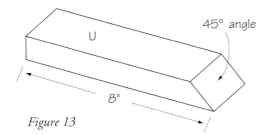

Figure 13

WOODEN DOORMAT

This oversized striped doormat is not only attractive but extremely practical. Debris can easily be scraped off the soles of shoes, and the weather-resistant wood can be hosed off with water. The doormat also provides sure footing during rain because water runs into the spaces between the wooden strips.

Materials and Supplies

50 linear feet of 1 x 2 pine
10 linear feet of 1 x 4 pine

Hardware

300   3d x 1¼" nails

Cutting List

Code	Description	Qty.	Materials	Dimensions
A	Long Side	2	1 x 2 pine	34½" long
B	Short Side	2	1 x 2 pine	24½" long
C	Narrow Support	6	1 x 2 pine	23" long
D	Wide Support	2	1 x 4 pine	23" long
E	Narrow Slat	9	1 x 2 pine	34½" long
F	Wide Slat	2	1 x 4 pine	34½" long

Making the Frame

1. Cut two long sides (A) from 1 x 2 pine, each measuring 34½ inches long.

2. Cut two short sides (B) from 1 x 2 pine, each measuring 24½ inches long.

3. Place the two short sides (B) on a level surface, parallel to each other and 34½ inches apart. Fit the two long sides (A) between the two short sides (B), as shown in figure 1. Nail through the short sides (B) into the ends of the long sides (A), using two 1½-inch-long nails on each joint.

Adding the Support Boards

4. Cut six narrow supports (C) from 1 x 2 pine, each measuring 23 inches long.

5. Cut two wide supports (D) from 1 x 4 pine, each measuring 23 inches long.

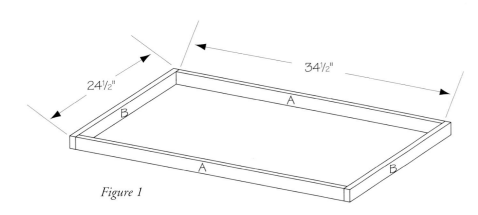

Figure 1

6. Place the frame assembly on a level surface. Refer to figure 2 to fit the narrow and wide supports (C and D) inside the frame assembly, placing the two wide supports (D) in the center of the frame, and three narrow supports (C) on each side of the wide supports (D). All the supports should be flush with the bottom of the frame assembly, ¾ inch from the top of the frame assembly, and approximately 2½ inches apart. The exact spacing is not critical. Nail through the long sides (A) into the ends of the narrow and wide supports (C and D).

Adding the Top Slats

7. Cut nine narrow slats (E) from 1 x 2 pine, each measuring 34½ inches long.

8. Cut two wide slats (F) from 1 x 4 pine, each measuring 34½ inches long.

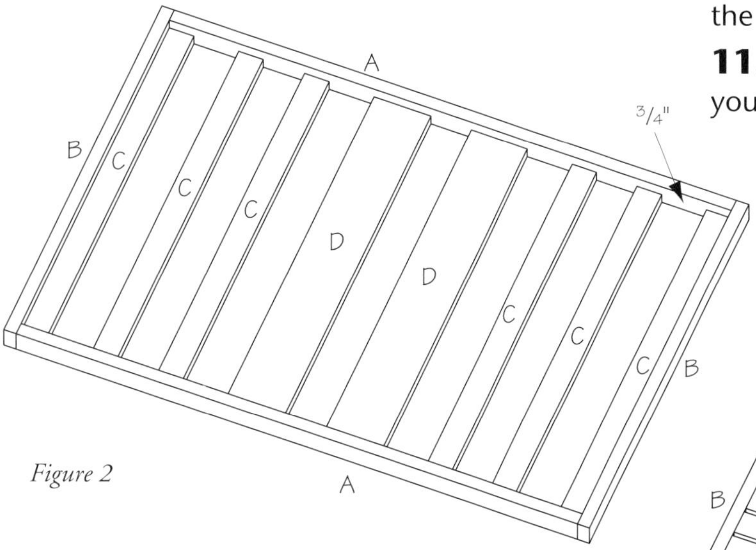

Figure 2

9. Place the frame assembly on a level surface. Refer to figure 3 to position the narrow and wide slats (E and F) inside the frame assembly. First, place one narrow slat (E) in the center, then two wide slats (F) on either side, then four more narrow slats (E) on each side. All the supports should be flush with the top of the frame assembly and ½ inch apart. The outer two narrow slats (E) should be flush with the long sides (A). Apply glue to the meeting surfaces, and nail through the long sides (A) into the ends of the narrow and wide slats (E and F). Then nail through each of the narrow and wide slats (E and F) into each of the narrow and wide supports (C and D)

Finishing

10. Fill any cracks, crevices, or screw holes with wood filler, and thoroughly sand all surfaces of the completed doormat.

11. Seal or stain your doormat the color of your choice.

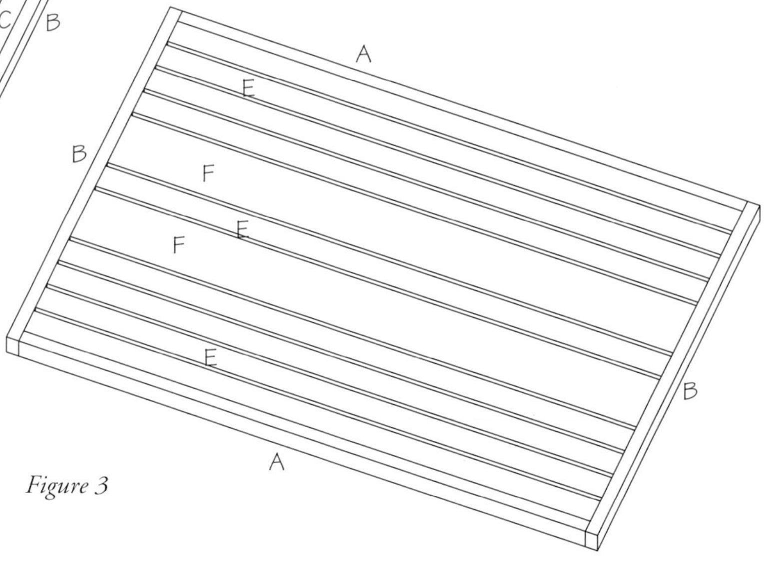

Figure 3

HAMMOCK STAND

If you've always wanted to have a hammock in your backyard, but couldn't because your trees weren't in the right place, here's the solution: No, you don't have to dig up two trees and replant them! Build this sturdy hammock stand instead, hang your favorite hammock on it, and place it anywhere you want—preferably where no one will disturb you!

Special Tools and Techniques

Dadoes

Miters

Materials and Supplies

44 linear feet of 4 x 4 pine

2 fencepost finials

Hardware

40	3" screws
40	2" screws
2	5⁄16" x 4" bolts, with 4 washers and 2 nuts
2	T-shaped metal back plates, 4" wide
2	metal screw hangers (sturdy enough to hold a hammock and two adults)

Cutting List (for both stands)

CODE	DESCRIPTION	QTY.	MATERIALS	DIMENSIONS
A	Cross Tie	2	4 x 4 pine	80" long
B	Upright	2	4 x 4 pine	56½" long
C	Front Brace	2	4 x 4 pine	33½" long
D	Side Brace	4	4 x 4 pine	12" long
E	Footing	2	4 x 4 pine	60" long

Cutting the Pieces

Each stand consists of two identical pieces constructed of 4 x 4 pine. Its strength comes from the system of dadoes cut into the individual pieces. It's not difficult to do, but requires some patience and rechecking to make certain that each of the boards is properly shaped. Take your time and work carefully, and all the pieces will fit together perfectly. The following are instructions for making one stand. Two stands will be required; if you wish to make them both at the same time, simply repeat each step.

1. Cut one cross tie (A) from 4 x 4 pine, measuring 80 inches long.

2. Follow figure 1 to measure and then cut a lap dado across the width of one end of the cross tie (A), 3½ inches across and 1¾ inches deep.

3. As shown in figure 1, cut a 45-degree diagonal dado in the cross tie (A), 12 inches from the lap dado, 3½ inches wide and 1¾ inches deep. Figure 1 shows an additional 12-inch-long dado cut on the remaining end. *This dado will be cut later.*

4. Cut one upright (B) from 4 x 4 pine, measuring 56½ inches long.

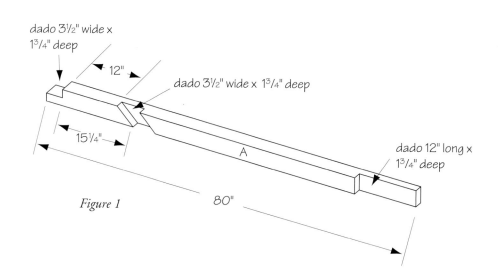

dado 3½" wide x 1³⁄4" deep

12"

dado 3½" wide x 1³⁄4" deep

15¼"

A

dado 12" long x 1³⁄4" deep

Figure 1   80"

5. Follow figure 2 to measure and then cut one 45-degree diagonal dado 3½ inches wide and 1¾ inches deep, 12 inches from what will be the bottom of the upright support (B).

6. Cut one front brace (C) from 4 x 4 pine, measuring 33½ inches long.

7. Miter both ends of the front brace (C) at opposing 45-degree angles, as shown in figure 3.

8. Cut two opposing diagonal dadoes in the front brace (C), 3½ inches wide and 1¾ inches deep, as shown in figure 4.

9. Cut two side braces (D) from 4 x 4 pine, each measuring 12 inches long.

10. Miter both ends of the side braces (D) at opposing 45-degree angles in the same manner as you did with the front braces (C), shown in figure 3.

11. Cut one footing (E) from 4 x 4 pine, measuring 60 inches long.

12. Follow figure 5 to cut a 3½-inch-wide dado, 1¾ inches deep, in the center of the footing (E).

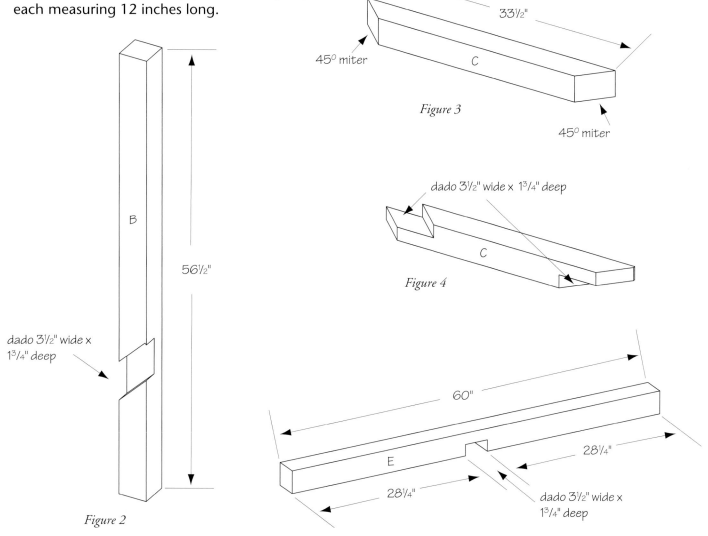

Figure 2

Figure 3

Figure 4

Figure 5

Assembling the Stand

13. Place the cross tie (A) on a level surface, with the lap dado exposed on the top, as shown in figure 1, page 110.

14. Place the footing (E) dado side down, over the lap dado in the cross tie (A). Screw them together by screwing through the footing dado into the cross tie dado. Use four 3-inch-long screws to secure the joint.

15. Fit the front brace (C) into the diagonal dado cut into the upright (B), as shown in figure 6.

16. Refer to figure 7 to complete the final steps of the assembly. Place the upright (B) directly over the dado joining the footing (E) and the cross-tie (A). Fit the free end of the front brace (C) into the diagonal dado cut in the cross tie (A). *Do not secure the joint yet.*

17. Place the metal back plate, "T" down, over the joint between the upright (B) and the footing (D), so that the side brackets extend around the upright. Screw the back plate to the footing using 2-inch-long screws through the back plate into the footing.

18. Make certain that the upright is exactly square to both the footing and the cross tie. First, screw through the metal back plate to secure the upright in place. Then, screw through the dado joint in the cross tie (A) and front brace (C), using four 3-inch-long screws. Finally, screw through the dado joint in the upright (B) and front brace (C), using four 3-inch-long screws.

19. Place one side brace (D), short side down, against the footing (E) and upright (A). Screw through one end of the side brace (D) into the footing (E) and through the other end of the side brace (D) into the upright (A). Use two 3-inch-long screws on each joint.

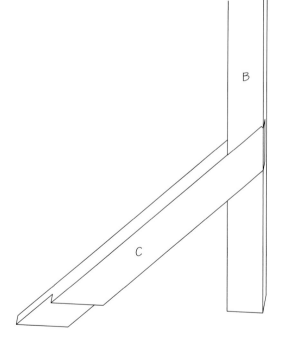

Figure 6

Figure 7

20. Repeat step 19 to attach the remaining side brace (D) to the opposite side of the upright (A) and footing (E).

21. Repeat steps 1 through 20 to make the second stand.

Finishing

22. Screw a metal hanger into each of the uprights (A), about 5 inches from the top, on the same side as the front brace (C).

23. The ends of the cross ties now must be marked and cut depending upon the size of your hammock. Place the two stands opposite each other, with the ends of the cross ties side by side. Hang your hammock on the hangers between the two stands. Move the two stands closer or farther apart, depending upon the size of your hammock, and how far from the ground you wish the hammock to hang. IT IS NOT SAFE TO GET IN THE HAMMOCK YET!

24. When you have decided what length the cross ties (A) should be, mark the length on the cross ties (A), and then mark a 12-inch length for overlap on each cross tie (A) Cut the cross ties (A) to length.

25. Remember the additional dado shown on the cross tie (A) shown in figure 1 (page 110)? Well, now is the time to cut it. Cut a 12-inch-long dado 1¾ inch deep in both cross ties, making certain that they are mirror images of each other.

26. Clamp the two dadoes together, and 3 inches from each end of the joint, drill two holes through both dadoes, large enough to accommodate your 4-inch bolts.

27. Place a washer on each bolt, fit the bolts through the drilled holes, add a second washer and a nut, and tighten the nuts.

28. Mark the center of the top of each upright, and screw in a decorative fencepost finial.

29. We left our hammock stand unfinished, but if you wish a more formal look, fill any cracks, crevices, or screw holes with wood filler, and thoroughly sand all surfaces.

30. Paint or stain the finished project the color of your choice, or simply seal it with a clear sealer.

31. Climb in your hammock and take a nap.

LAWN BENCH

This versatile lawn bench can serve a multitude of purposes. We've used it as a bench for seating, as an outdoor coffee table, and even to hold a collection of plants. It's easy to make, and very sturdy when completed.

Materials and Supplies

30 linear feet of 1 x 4 pine
22 linear feet of 1 x 2
10 linear feet of 2 x 2 pine

Hardware

60   3d x 1¼" nails
15   4d x 1½" nails
30   1¼" screws
30   1⅝" screws
20   2½" screws

Cutting List

Code	Description	Qty.	Materials	Dimensions
A	Long Top	2	1 x 4	53" long
B	Short Top	2	1 x 4	14" long
C	Leg	4	2 x 2	16¼" long
D	Long Inner Support	2	1 x 2	48½" long
E	Slat	14	1 x 4	14" long
F	Leg Brace	2	2 x 2	11" long
G	Lower Support	2	1 x 2	48½" long
H	Spacer	3	1 x 2	2¼" long

Constructing the Bench Top

1. Cut two long tops (A) from 1 x 4 pine, each measuring 53 inches long.

2. Cut two short tops (B) from 1 x 4 pine, each measuring 14 inches long.

3. Place the two short tops (B) between the ends of the long tops (A), as shown in figure 1. Screw through the long tops (A) into the ends of the short tops (B), using two 1⅝-inch-long screws on each joint.

Adding the Legs

4. Cut four legs (C) from 2 x 2 pine, each measuring 16¼ inches long.

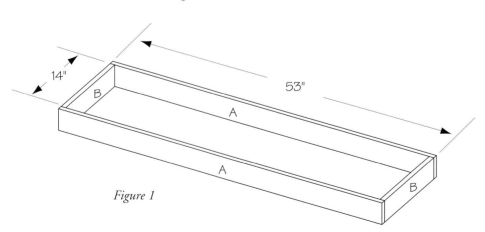

Figure 1

5. Attach each of the four legs to the four inner corners of the top assembly, ¾ inch from the top edges of the long and short tops (A and B), as shown in figure 2. Screw through the long and short tops (A and B) into the legs (C), using two 1⅝-inch-long screws in each side of the legs (C).

Adding the Inner Supports

6. Cut two long inner supports (D) from 1 x 2 pine, each measuring 48½ inches long.

7. Attach one long inner support (D) to the inside of the one long top (A), as shown in figure 3. It should be positioned flush with the top of the leg (C), ¾ inch from the top edge of the long top (A). Screw through the long inner support (D) into the long top (A), using 1¼-inch-long screws, approximately every six inches.

8. Repeat step 6 to attach the remaining long inner support (D) to the inside of the opposite long top (A).

Adding the Slats

9. Cut 14 slats (E) from 1 x 4 pine, each measuring 14 inches long.

10. Place the 14 slats (E) over the assembled inner supports, as shown in figure 4 on page 117. Space them evenly between the short tops (B), leaving a small space between slats. The exact measurement is not critical—just make certain that all the spaces are equal and that the slats are all straight. Nail through the ends of each of the slats into the long inner supports (D) and the legs (C), using two 1¼-inch-long nails on each end.

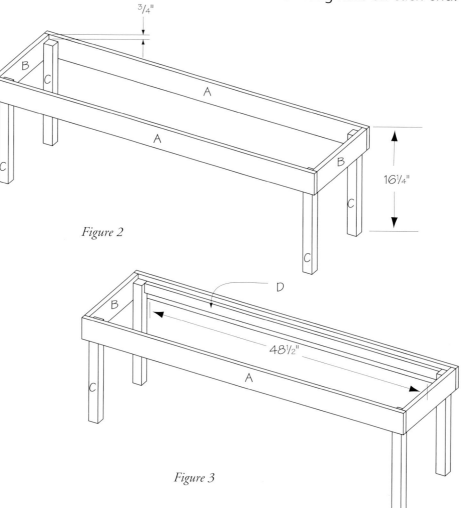

Figure 2

Figure 3

Adding the Leg Supports

11. Cut two leg braces (F) from 2 x 2 pine, each measuring 11 inches long.

12. Attach a leg brace (F) between two of the legs (C), 8 inches from the bottom, as shown in figure 4. Screw through the legs (C) into the ends of the leg braces (F), using two 2½-inch-long screws on each joint.

13. Repeat step 12 to attach the other leg brace (F) between the opposite legs (C).

Adding the Lower Support

14. Cut two lower supports (G) from 1 x 2 pine, each measuring 48½ inches long.

15. Cut three spacers (H) from 1 x 2 pine, each measuring 2¼ inches long.

16. Place the two lower supports (G) on a level surface, parallel to each other, and 2½ inches

apart. Fit the three spacers (H) evenly between the two lower supports, just over 11½ inches apart, as shown in figure 5.

17. Nail through the two lower supports (G) into the ends of the spacers (H). Use two 1½-inch-long nails on each joint.

18. Fit the assembled lower support between the two leg braces (F), centering it on the braces. Screw through the leg braces (F) into the ends of the two lower supports (G). Use two 2½-inch-long screws on each joint.

Finishing the Bench

19. Fill any cracks, crevices, or screw holes with wood filler and thoroughly sand all surfaces of the lawn bench.

20. Seal and paint, or stain the completed bench the color of your choice. We left our project the natural color of the pressure-treated pine.

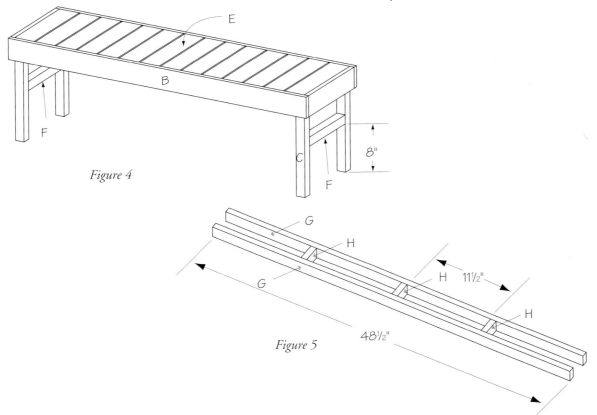

Figure 4

Figure 5

HURRICANE LAMPS

These easy-to-make lamps provide terrific lighting for outdoor evening meals, and they cost next to nothing to make. We painted our pair white, and stamped on a vine pattern. Combine them with your favorite candles, and they will add light and charm to backyard entertaining.

Materials and Supplies

Note: The following is enough material to make one hurricane lamp. Just double the amount to construct two.

5 linear feet of 1 x 4 pine

1 linear foot of 1 x 6 pine

One hurricane glass globe

Primer

Base paint

Trim paint

Paintbrushes

Stamp in a motif of your choice

Clear, waterproof sealer

Hardware

20   3d x 1¼" nails

Cutting List

CODE	DESCRIPTION	QTY.	MATERIALS	DIMENSIONS
A	Side	4	1 x 4 pine	12" long
B	Top/Bottom	2	1 x 6 pine	5½" long
C	Candle Holder	1	1 x 4 pine	2" long

Constructing the Lamp

1. Cut four sides (A) from 1 x 4 pine, each measuring 12 inches long.

2. Assemble the four sides (A), overlapping each piece in rotation, as shown in figure 1. With the four sides (A) in position, the stand measures 4¼ inches wide on all sides. Apply glue to the meeting surfaces, and nail all four sides (A) along their entire length. Use 1¼-inch-long nails spaced about four inches apart.

3. Cut two top/bottoms (B) from 1 x 6 pine, measuring 5½ inches long.

4. Center one top/bottom (B) over the assembled sides (A). Nail through the top/bottom (B) into the sides (A).

5. Cut one candle holder (C) from 1 x 4 pine, 2 x 2 inches square. Drill a candle-sized hole (ours was ¾ inch in diameter) in the center of the 2-inch square. Trim the corners of the square, as shown in figure 2, so that the candle holder fits inside the bottom of the hurricane glass.

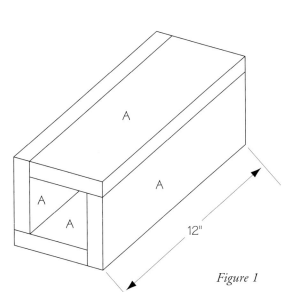

Figure 1

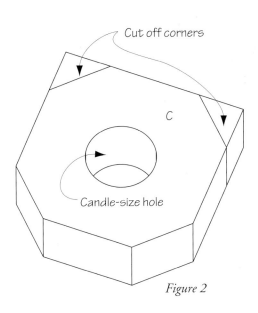

Cut off corners

Candle-size hole

Figure 2

6. Center the candle holder (C) over the remaining top/bottom (B). Apply glue to the meeting surfaces, and nail through the candle holder (C) into the top/bottom (B). Use four 1¼-inch-long nails (one in each corner).

7. Turn the assembled sides (A) right side up. Center the top/bottom (B) with the attached candle holder (C) over the assembled sides (A). Nail through the top/bottom (B) into the sides (A).

Finishing

8. Fill any cracks, crevices, or nail holes with wood filler, and thoroughly sand all surfaces of the completed lamp.

9. We primed and painted our lamps white, then stamped on an ivy pattern. There are many different types of stamps available in craft- and hobby-supply stores, so you should be able to find an ivy motif like this one, or choose a pattern to match your own table decor. Be sure that your trim paint is compatible with your base paint.

10. When the paint is dry, seal your completed lamp to protect it from the elements.

CHAISE LOUNGE

This easy-to-make chaise lounge will become a favorite place for napping in the sun or reading a good book underneath a shade tree. Because it's on wheels, you can move it to any location you wish— even to the beach!

Special Tools and Techniques

Dadoes

Materials and Supplies

30 linear feet of 2 x 4 pine

45 linear feet of 1 x 4 pine

25 linear feet of 1 x 2 pine

2 linear feet of 1"-wide dowel rod

Hardware

60	1¼" screws
12	1½" screws
15	2½" screws
50	3d x 1¼" nails
50	4d x 1½" nails
2	⅜" x 2" carriage bolts with matching washers and nuts
2	⅜" x 3" carriage bolts with matching washers and nuts
2	½" x 4" machine bolts with matching washers and nuts
2	7"-diameter wheels (the type used for lawn mowers)

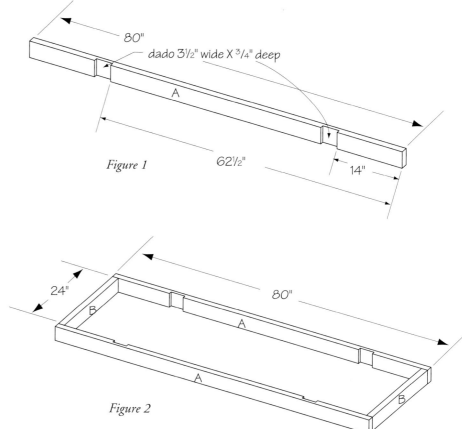

Figure 1

Figure 2

Cutting List

Code	Description	Qty.	Materials	Dimensions
A	Side	2	2 x 4 pine	80" long
B	Front/Back	2	2 x 4 pine	24" long
C	Front Leg	2	2 x 4 pine	14" long
D	Back Leg	2	2 x 4 pine	12" long
E	Leg Support	1	2 x 4 pine	24" long
F	Inner Support	2	1 x 2 pine	44" long
G	Slat	11	1 x 4 pine	24" long
H	Inner Rack	1	1 x 4 pine	19" long
I	Short Back Support	2	1 x 2 pine	22⅜" long
J	Long Back Support	2	1 x 2 pine	31½" long
K	Back Slat	8	1 x 4 pine	23⅞" long
L	Rod	1	1" dowel rod	23⅞" long
M	Extender	2	1 x 2 pine	15" long

Making the Frame

1. Cut two sides (A) from 2 x 4 pine, each measuring 80 inches long.

2. Cut two dadoes across the width of side (A), as shown in figure 1. Each dado is 3½ inches wide and ¾ inch deep.

3. Cut two front/backs (B) from 2 x 4 pine, each measuring 24 inches long.

4. Place the sides (A) on a level surface, parallel to each other and 24 inches apart. The dadoed surfaces should be facing each other. Place the two front/backs (B) between the two sides (A), as shown in figure 2. Screw through the sides (A) into the ends of the front/backs (B), using two 2½-inch-long screws on each joint.

Adding the Legs

5. Cut two front legs (C) from 2 x 4 pine, each measuring 14 inches long.

6. Cut a lap dado on one end of a front leg (C), measuring 3½ inches wide and ¾ inches deep, as shown in figure 3. Repeat the procedure to cut a lap dado on the remaining front leg (C).

7. Apply glue to the meeting surfaces and fit the dado in one front leg (C) into the dado 14 inches from the end of one side (A), as shown in figure 4. Screw through the dadoed portions of both the front leg (C) and side (A), using two 1¼-inch-long screws on each side of the joint. Repeat the procedure to attach the remaining front leg (C) to the opposite side (A).

8. Cut two back legs (D) from 2 x 4 pine, each measuring 12 inches long.

9. Cut a lap dado on one end of a back leg (D), measuring 3½ inches wide and ¾ inches deep, as shown in figure 5.

10. Drill a ½-inch hole through the opposite end of the back leg (D). The hole should be centered on the wide surface of the back leg (D), and 1½ inches from the end of the back leg (D).

11. Repeat steps 9 and 10 to cut a lap dado and drill a bolt hole in the remaining back leg (D).

12. Apply glue to the meeting surfaces and fit the dado in one back leg (D) into one of the remaining dadoes in the side (A), as shown in figure 4. Screw through the dadoed portions of both the back leg (D) and side (A), using two 1¼-inch-long screws on each side of the joint. Repeat this procedure to attach the remaining back leg (D).

13. Cut one leg support (E) from 2 x 4 pine, measuring 24 inches long.

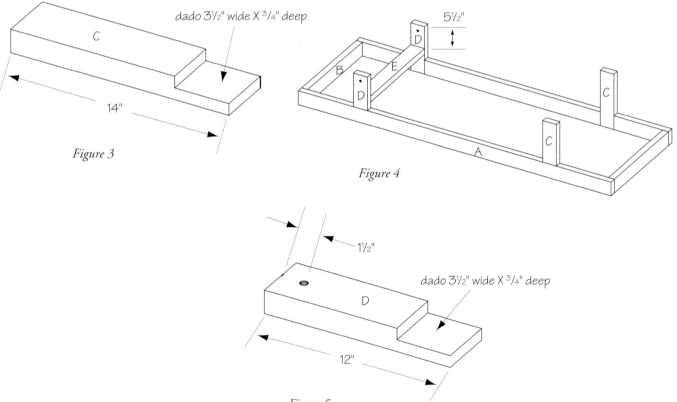

dado 3½" wide X ¾" deep

14"

Figure 3

5½"

Figure 4

1½"

dado 3½" wide X ¾" deep

12"

Figure 5

14. Fit the leg support (E) between the two back legs (D), 5½ inches from the bottom of the leg, as shown in figure 4 on page 123. Screw through the back legs (D) into the end of the leg support (E), using two 2½-inch-long screws on each joint.

Adding the Front Slats

15. The chaise consists of two parts: the front leg area, which is stationary; and the backrest area, which is adjustable. The front leg area consists of slats set over inner supports. Cut two long inner supports (F) from 1 x 2 pine, each measuring 44 inches long.

16. Apply glue to the meeting surfaces and attach one inner support (F) ¾ inch below the top edge of the inner side (A), as shown in figure 6. Screw through the inner support (F) and into the side (A), using 1¼-inch-long screws spaced about every 4 or 5 inches. Repeat this procedure to attach the second inner support (F) to the opposite inner side (A).

Adding the Slats

17. Cut 11 slats (G) from 1 x 4 pine, each measuring 24 inches long.

18. Attach one slat (G) over the inner supports (F), ½ inch from the front/back (B), as shown in figure 7. Nail through the end of the slat (G) into the inner supports (F). Use two 1¼-inch-long nails on each joint.

19. Repeat the same procedure to attach the remaining 10 slats (G) on top of the inner supports (F), spacing each slat ½ inch from the previous one.

Making the Inner Rack

20. The angle of the chaise back is adjusted by placing a wooden rod into your choice of multiple slots in the inner rack. Cut one inner rack (H) from 1 x 4 pine, measuring 19 inches long.

21. Drill six 1-inch-diameter holes 2 inches apart along the length of the inner rack (H), beginning 1½ inches from the end, as shown in figure 8. These holes must be centered widthwise on the 1 x 4.

22. Cut the inner rack (H) in half lengthwise along the dotted lines shown in figure 8, cutting through the center of all six drilled holes. The resulting two half-pieces will now provide the slots for the chaise back adjustment.

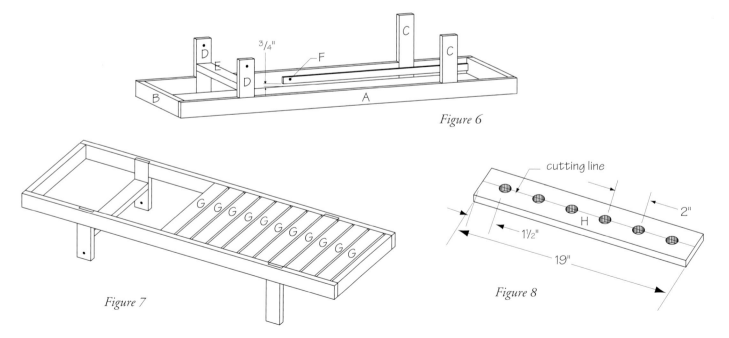

Figure 6

Figure 7

Figure 8

23. Attach one half-piece (drilled half-circles up) 2¼ inches from the top of the lower edge of side (A), 1½ inches from the front/back (B), as shown in figure 9. Note that the half-piece will extend below the lower edge of side (A). Apply glue to the meeting surfaces, and use four evenly spaced 1½-inch-long screws along the length to attach the inner rack (H) to the side (A). Repeat this procedure to attach the remaining half-piece (H) to the opposite side (A).

Making the Chaise Back

24. Cut two short back supports (I) from 1 x 2 pine, each measuring 22⅜ inches long.

25. Cut two long back supports (J) from 1 x 2 pine, each measuring 31½ inches long.

26. Measure 13½ inches from one end of each long back support (J) and center a mark on the wide face. Drill a ¾-inch countersink ¼ inch deep. Then drill a ⅜-inch hole through the back support (J), as shown in figure 10.

27. Place the two long back supports (J) on a flat surface, parallel to each other and 22⅜ inches apart. Fit the two short back supports (I) between the two long back supports (K), as shown in figure 10. Nail through the long back supports (J) into the ends of the short back supports (I), using two 1½-inch-long nails on each joint.

28. Cut eight back slats (K) from 1 x 4 pine, each measuring 23⅞ inches long.

29. Fit the back slats (K) over the assembled frame, spacing them ½ inch apart, in the same manner that you used to attach the 11 slats (G). Nail through the end of the back slats (K) into the edges of the two long inner supports. Use two 1½-inch-long nails on each joint.

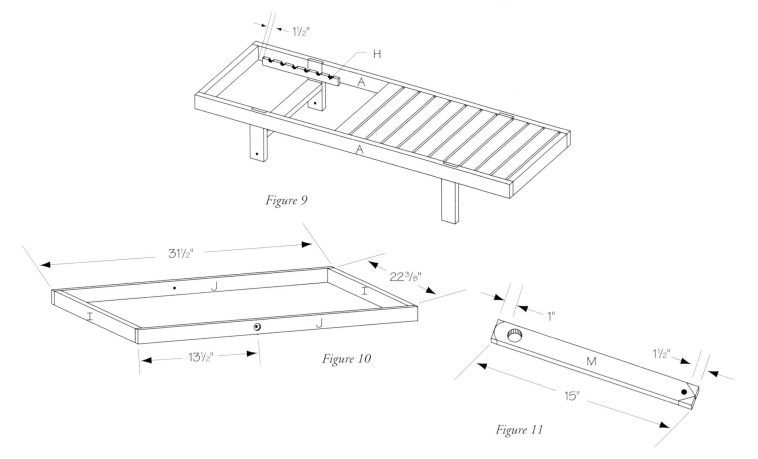

Figure 9

Figure 10

Figure 11

Making the Rod Assembly

30. Cut one rod (L) from 1-inch-diameter dowel rod to a length of 23⅞ inches.

31. Cut two extenders (M) from 1 x 2 pine, each measuring 15 inches long.

32. Drill a 1-inch-diameter hole through one end of one extender (M), as shown in figure 11 on page 125. Then round off the end of the extender around the hole that you just drilled.

33. Shape the opposite end of the extender (M) by cutting off both corners, and drill a ⅜-inch hole in that same end, as shown in figure 11.

34. Thread the rod (L) through the 1-inch holes you drilled in each of the extenders (M). Make certain that the rod length on each side of the extenders is equal. Then nail through each extender into the rod, using a 1½-inch-long nail.

35. Place the extenders inside the chaise back, matching the drilled holes. Secure them by inserting a 2-inch-long bolt through the chaise back and then through the extender (M). Add a washer and nut, and tighten securely.

36. The finished chaise consists of the assembled back portion, which can be raised or lowered, and the slats that accommodate the legs. A hole must be drilled through the chaise and the back assembly to accommodate a bolt that enables the back to be raised and lowered.

To add the back portion to the assembled chaise, place the assembled chaise upside down on a level surface. Holding the assembled chaise back upside down, fit it underneath the leg support (E), between the two sides (A), so that the back slats (K) rest against the work surface, as shown in figure 12. Clamp the long back supports (J) to the sides (A) to hold them securely while you drill a hole.

Measure down 32 inches from the rear of the chaise on side (A), and drill a hole through both sides (A) and through the long back support (J), large enough to accommodate a 3-inch-long bolt. Insert the bolt through the side (A) and through the long back support (J). Add a washer and nut, and tighten securely.

Finishing

37. Thread a washer over a 4-inch bolt. Then fit the bolt through one wheel and through the drilled hole in the back leg (D). Add a washer and nut, and tighten. Repeat this procedure to attach the remaining wheel to the opposite back leg (D).

38. Thoroughly sand the completed chaise.

39. We wanted a natural appearance for our chaise so we didn't even fill the holes. However, if you wish a more finished look, fill all of the screw holes and cracks with wood filler, and sand again. You can leave the chaise its natural color or stain or paint it whatever color you wish.

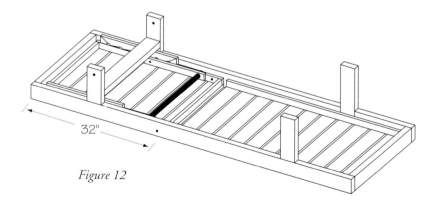

Figure 12

CONVERSION CHART

Inches	CM		Inches	CM
⅛	0.3		20	50.8
¼	0.6		21	53.3
⅜	1.0		22	55.9
½	1.3		23	58.4
⅝	1.6		24	61.0
¾	1.9		25	63.5
⅞	2.2		26	66.0
1	2.5		27	68.6
1¼	3.2		28	71.1
1½	3.8		29	73.7
1¾	4.4		30	76.2
2	5.1		31	78.7
2½	6.4		32	81.3
3	7.6		33	83.8
3½	8.9		34	86.4
4	10.2		35	88.9
4½	11.4		36	91.4
5	12.7		37	94.0
6	15.2		38	96.5
7	17.8		39	99.1
8	20.3		40	101.6
9	22.9		41	104.1
10	25.4		42	106.7
11	27.9		43	109.2
12	30.5		44	111.8
13	33.0		45	114.3
14	35.6		46	116.8
15	38.1		47	119.4
16	40.6		48	121.9
17	43.2		49	124.5
18	45.7		50	127.0
19	48.3			

ACKNOWLEDGMENTS

We gratefully acknowledge the assistance of many people who deserve credit for the successful production of this book. Many thanks to:

-**Evan Bracken** (Light Reflections, Hendersonville, NC), who once again triumphed over a four-day photography shoot. Thanks for your talent and patience!

-**Deborah Morgenthal** (Lark Books, Asheville, NC), my editor, whose skill, patience, and kindness got us through this project.

-**Kathy Holmes** (Lark Books, Asheville, NC), my art director, for designing a beautiful and user-friendly book.

-**Thomas Stender** (Chicago, IL) for turning my sketches into professional-looking illustrations, and for catching our mistakes.

-To the following people who assisted with photography and let us tramp around and through their property and lives; they are (in alphabetical order) **Jack Bergbom, Jessica Diehl, Debbie** and **Maurice Droulers, Charlene Foy, Phil Goldman, Patti Kertz, Benny** and **Becky Parrish, Carrie** and **Marty Shindler,** and **Phil Winkelspecht.** Thanks for giving up your sanity and your space to make this book better!

INDEX